XAIVER MICHAEL CAMPBELL
HEATHER BARRETT

BLACK HARBOUR

SLAVERY AND THE FORGOTTEN HISTORIES OF BLACK PEOPLE IN NEWFOUNDLAND AND LABRADOR

BOULDER
BOOKS

Library and Archives Canada Cataloguing in Publication

Title: Black harbour : slavery and the forgotten histories
of Black people in Newfoundland and
    Labrador / Xaiver Michael Campbell, Heather Barrett.
Names: Barrett, Heather (Journalist), author. | Campbell, Xaiver Michael, author.
Identifiers: Canadiana 20230505589 | ISBN 9781989417867 (hardcover)
Subjects: LCSH: Slavery—Newfoundland and Labrador. | LCSH: Black people—
Newfoundland and Labrador—History. | CSH: Black Canadians—Newfoundland
    and Labrador—History.
Classification: LCC HT1052.N6 B37 2023 | DDC 306.3/6209718—dc23

© 2023 Xaiver Michael Campbell, Heather Barrett

Published by Boulder Books
Portugal Cove-St. Philip's, Newfoundland and Labrador
www.boulderbooks.ca

Design and layout: Tanya Montini
Editor: Stephanie Porter
Copy editor: Iona Bulgin

Printed in Canada

Excerpts from this publication may be reproduced under licence from Access
Copyright, or with the express written permission of Boulder Books Ltd.,
or as permitted by law. All rights are otherwise reserved and no part of this
publication may be reproduced, stored in a retrieval system, or transmitted
in any form or by any means, electronic, mechanical, photocopying, scanning,
recording, or otherwise, except as specifically authorized.

We acknowledge the financial support of the Government of Newfoundland and
Labrador through the Department of Tourism, Culture, Arts and Recreation.

For Sarah, Rachel, Nancy, Sancho, Stephen, Katherine, Dinah, Rachel, Cornelius, and W.H.

Contents

Land and Labour Acknowledgments 6
Preface 9
Fate Finds a Way with Xaiver 13
Heather Goes to Black Harbour 17
Who Was W.H.? 20
The Almighty Cod 24
Enslavement and the Triangular Trade 27
Xaiver Chats Cod 31
Heather Goes to Lagos 35
Black Sailors 40
Black Slavery in Canada 44
Xaymaca and Spanish Conquest 48
The Streets of St. John's 50
The Bermudian Interruption 53
Early Newfoundland 57
Colonies 60
Jamaica: Rebellions and British Rule 62
Calvert's Ferryland 67
Kirke's Ferryland 71
Benger's Ferryland 75
No Fairy Tales in Ferryland 77
Domestic Property 83
Dinah, Cornelius, and Rachel 86
Enslaved Domestics 90

Slave Ships 93
The *Sarah*. 97
Quieted Community Affairs 101
Emancipation. 107
Jamaica's Journey: Abolition to Independence 109
What Now?. 112
The Cod Endures 114
The Thing about Fish. 116
Kevin Toope's Salt Fish 120
Colonial Foodways Today 125
Heather Bakes 128
M'lasses. 131
Foodways and Memories 134
Come From Away. 139
New Frames for Newfoundland. 145
Heather Reframes 148
Xaiver Rethinks 151
Revisiting W.H. 154
Dear W.H. 157

Black Harbour Timeline: Newfoundland and Labrador 159
Black Harbour Timeline: Jamaica 163
References and Further Reading 168
Appendix 1: Newfoundland-Built Ships in the
    Transatlantic Slave Trade 174
Appendix 2: Newfoundland-Built Ships in
    the Intra-American Slave Trade 178
Acknowledgements 180
About the Authors 182

Land Acknowledgement

We respectfully acknowledge that we live and work on the stolen ancestral homelands of the Beothuk nation and communities, whose culture has been lost forever.

We acknowledge the island of Ktaqmkuk (Newfoundland) as the unceded, traditional territory of the Beothuk and the Mi'kmaq nations and communities. We acknowledge Labrador as the traditional and ancestral homelands of the Innu of Nitassinan, the Inuit of Nunatsiavut, and the Inuit of NunatuKavut.

We are indepted to all First People who were here before us, those who live with us now, and for the seven generations to come.

As First Peoples have done since time immemorial, we strive to be responsible stewards of the land and to respect the cultures, ceremonies, and traditions of all who call it home.

As we write, we open our hearts and minds to the past, and we commit to moving forward in a spirit of truth and reconciliation to make a better future for all.

Labour Acknowledgement

We graciously acknowledge the labour of enslaved Africans who suffered the horrors of transatlantic trafficking and unwillingly gave to the building of the Canadian nation state and other global economies, including shipbuilding and codfishing in Newfoundland and Labrador.

We are indebted to their labour and their sacrifice, and we must acknowledge the tremors of that violence throughout the generations and the resulting impact that can still be felt and witnessed today.

We honour all those who made it through the Middle Passage and those who did not.

Preface

Xaiver: Heather, I wonder if it was fate that our paths crossed?

Heather: Xaiver, I'm so glad I met you! I didn't know if anyone else was wondering about whether Black people were around Newfoundland and Labrador over the centuries.

Xaiver: After all my years living in Newfoundland and Labrador, I've wondered if the similarities between my island of Jamaica and your island of Newfoundland are just coincidental. Or if they go back to deeper connections that people do not often talk about.

Heather: Jamaican rum has always been popular around here. I never stopped to wonder why. My kitchen cupboard always has molasses in it. I just figured everyone's kitchen cupboard has molasses.

Xaiver: Ironically enough, so did mine. I often drove by sugar cane fields on the way to the countryside. It was Jamaica, after all. My grandma rubbed rum on my gums as a baby to ease teething pains, and it's probably the most important ingredient in our fruitcake.

Heather: Fruitcake? I love dark rum fruitcake. And I'm surprised that we both grew up with salt cod.

Xaiver: It's these connections and more that led us to wonder what else links us that we don't talk about. Like the peoples who ensured that the world had these products. How they lived, where they lived, and how they made it to the New World.

Heather: Here in Newfoundland and Labrador, we frequently speak about the struggles of the early English, Irish, and French settlers. It never occurred to me to think who else may have sailed into our ports and under what circumstances.

Xaiver: I never stopped to think that people beyond those English, Irish, and French settlers lived here, had families, contributed to the culture and the future generations of Newfoundlanders and Labradorians. That some of these people were Black people, freed and enslaved. These people were here.

Heather: We're opening an ocean-sized can of worms.

Xaiver: I think it's the right time. We're able to talk to experts who also enjoy opening cans of worms. People who've made it their duty to disturb the status quo.

Heather: I'm not an expert or an historian. I'm a journalist, and I love to ask questions.

Xaiver: I'm also not a journalist, or an expert, by any means. I'm passionate about telling stories about Newfoundland and Newfoundlanders, because I now consider myself one. I feel like the range of stories that can be told about this island, from its origins as a colony until today, has expanded. We can talk about Black people as Newfoundlanders, as parts of the culture that we love.

Heather: It's exciting to consider who else came here and helped create what's now our homeland. But I'm not going to lie; I'm a bit nervous. Some of what we find out is difficult to think about.

Xaiver: We've been expertly guided by historians, artists, archaeologists, professors, salt-fish experts, and so many others to help us paint a more diverse early Newfoundland and Labrador than what we are often privy to or have been taught. Our goal is to add to the Newfoundland history we know. I'd also like to look at what was going on in Jamaica while we explore what happened in Newfoundland over the past few centuries. We still don't know the whole story; we just want to start the conversation.

Heather: So, are we ready to set sail to Black Harbour?

Xaiver: We may not be ready. But we're going. Let's connect some dots.

Fate Finds a Way with Xaiver

XMC

As a Jamaican, I knew that the same salt fish I enjoyed cooked with ackee, or beans, or fresh coconut milk from birth in 1989 was the same fish my enslaved ancestors ate so they could work the cane fields to make sugar, molasses, and rum. We were all privy to this knowledge in Jamaica. Our history, the trials we had to endure as a people at the hand of our English colonizers, was taught to us. Our national heroes manifested those struggles and were celebrated for it.

At 19, I moved to Newfoundland. An island in the middle of the North Atlantic Ocean. It was cold and windy, and leagues from everything I had known as a Caribbean islander. But not everything was different. I learned quickly that this Canadian province, once its own country, was a former British colony and that some of our traditions were similar. The names varied, and the flavours, but the spirit and ingredients were the same. One of those traditions was salt fish. Salt cod. Cod.

In my first year in Newfoundland, an elderly sailor handed me a photograph of the Blue Mountains in Jamaica. He had been on board the MV *Placentia*, a Newfoundland vessel, after it had made a salt-fish delivery to Jamaica in 1948. He regaled me with his sea travels and the joy he felt sailing into Kingston harbour to deliver fish: the excitement of the locals, some of whom would swim out to meet them, while others waited excitedly to help unload. All for the salt fish. That was when I learned that cod had linked Jamaica and Newfoundland for centuries before Newfoundland joined Canada.

The photograph of the Kingston, Jamaica, waterfront given to Xaiver. On the reverse is inscribed: *Taken from the deck of the MV Placentia in June 1948. We were leaving for Turk's Island, having discharged 325 tons of Nfld salt codfish.*

In all my years in Jamaica, I never wondered where the dried, emaciated slices of paper-thin fish originated. But now I lived in the place it came from. The cod in the water surrounding my new home was the cod that my grandmother grew up eating. The same cod, from the same place, also fed my enslaved ancestors.

I would not have guessed that my new home of Newfoundland, Canada, so far in the North Atlantic Ocean, with its mostly Irish, English, and French heritage, would have anything to do with the transatlantic slave trade. Or that I, a Black Jamaican, might have any connection to this island before I even arrived.

Before I stepped off the plane in St. John's, I was warned not to expect to see anyone who looked like me. It was 2008 and the lore of there being no Black people in Newfoundland was alive and thriving. Even though that was not the case. I landed, and as the new day dawned, I saw faces like mine crossing the campus of Memorial University of Newfoundland, now Memorial University of Newfoundland and Labrador. The scrubbing of Black people from the Newfoundland citizenry has lingering, mature, deep roots. As I have now lived here longer, I have wondered if people were right in the historical sense: had there never been Black people in Newfoundland? Did Black slavery not crash on the shores of Newfoundland during the centuries when it was legal in all British colonies to enslave people that looked like me?

My interest piqued when I first had Screech and realized it was a version of the rum that I had grown up tasting in fruitcake; in the punch at celebrations; and in the kick in the sorrel (the dried hibiscus tea drunk at Christmas time in Jamaica). It tasted different but also the same. Jamaican rum was entrenched in the culture of this place. They baptized me in this liquid as if it were indigenous to them. How could this be? When did this begin? I thought again of the cod.

What was the known Newfoundland Black history? What had shaped the culture on the island? Without a celebrated or even widely known Newfoundland Black history had the connections between Newfoundland and the transatlantic slave trade been expunged?

I sat on these feelings for over a decade as I settled into my new life. I did two political science degrees. Majoring in Canadian politics and still nothing and no institution or person really told me what had happened between the two islands centuries ago or of the plight of the Indigenous people on their own lands. Upon a change in career to the telling of stories, this was one story I knew I needed to have a hand in telling. The surface had been scratched by others, but there is more to dig up and it was and is hard work.

My curiosity was met by other curious minds, including journalist Heather Barrett. By connecting to and working with Heather, who was entrenched in her own journey of uncovering Newfoundland's involvement in the transatlantic slave trade, we brought to the public some of our questions and answers in a CBC Radio documentary, *Unearthed*. It was invaluable being able to share with the residents of my new home something they might not have known about their own history. Brilliant artists, academics, and researchers such as Dr. Sonja Boon, Dr. Afua Cooper, Dr. Barry Gaulton, Dale Jarvis, Bushra Junaid, Dr. Neil Kennedy, and Dr. Camille Turner helped satisfy our curiosities with their knowledge.[1] This telling of Newfoundland and Labrador Black history is only possible because of the work being done by these experts.

Turner, when interviewed for that documentary, says that by doing this work we are "paying homage to the people who came before [us]." We, the living, get to remember those who were not remembered by history. This work "exposes the lies, the silences, the omissions, the erasures." Is it this erasure that has left Newfoundland Black history largely untold and forgotten for centuries? This book gives both Heather and me the chance to share our explorations. It also gives me a place where I can dream of the possible realities of Black bodies in Newfoundland and imagine the richness Black people have contributed to the culture of Newfoundland for centuries.

The same cod that fed me as a child fed my enslaved ancestors hundreds of years ago. It came from the same place: Newfoundland. And most importantly, I know that there were Black people, free and enslaved, present in early Newfoundland. But that is just the beginning.

---

1 These voices were all part of *Unearthed*.

Heather Goes to Black Harbour
HB

This all started on a July afternoon at my day job as a radio host and producer. I was recording an audio interview with Ngozi Paul, a Black Canadian actor and creator, who was discussing the new Canadian holiday on August 1, Emancipation Day. Emancipation Day marks the day in 1834 that the Slavery Abolition Act came into effect across the British empire, which abolished the enslavement of Black and Indigenous people.

Like many Canadians, I am learning more about Indigenous people and their experiences, but I had heard very little about enslaved Black people in Canada. I had assumed that the horrific transatlantic slave trade happened elsewhere, farther south: the United States, the Caribbean, and South America.

Then Paul said, "Wherever there was colonization, there was slavery."

Wait a minute. Newfoundland was a British colony until 1949, the year it joined Canada. European colonizers had come to Newfoundland and the southern Labrador shores to fish our waters for cod since about 1500.

Did that mean enslaved Black people came to Newfoundland and Labrador? Did that mean Newfoundland and Labrador was at least partially built on the labour of enslaved Black people? Did that mean that the history I was taught all my life—in school, in our folklore, in our songs and tales—left out a major part of Newfoundland and Labrador's story?

I started asking questions. The answer to all the above is *yes*.

I have been a journalist for several decades, most of that time working in Newfoundland and Labrador. Daily life in 21st-century Newfoundland and Labrador is deeply steeped in our history. It is a place, the stories go, that was founded by brave and hardy English and Irish souls. People who, despite the harsh weather, poor soil, and dangerous North Atlantic Ocean, were determined to build lives and communities.

Our work ethic, our sense of community, and our strong culture are products of those early difficult centuries.

The transatlantic slave trade does not come up in these tales.

When I was growing up in St. John's in the 1970s and 1980s, no Black people were present in our history books about Newfoundland and Labrador and about Canada. The only Black person I had ever seen *in person* was Richard, a high school classmate. For me, and almost everyone I knew, Black people, their history and their culture, were seen in American television shows or heard in American music. The Newfoundland and Labrador I was born and raised in was a sea of white.

My Barrett ancestors can be traced back to John Barrett, an Englishman who came to Old Perlican, a large fishing station, in Trinity Bay, Newfoundland, in 1711. Other branches of my family lived in the nearby Conception Bay communities of Carbonear and Grates Cove in the early 1800s.

I am a descendant of generations of Protestant fishing families, who originally came from the West Country of England. Our pale Barrett skin is prone to sunburn. Nowhere in our family tree, or community outport histories, is there mention of Black people.

All this is to say that I had never really considered the connections between Newfoundland and Labrador and the transatlantic slave trade. Our ancestors, struggling to survive on this rock, had it hard enough, did they not?

They did. But others had it harder.

As I continued to ask questions, and have conversations, I met Xaiver Michael Campbell, originally from Jamaica. Xaiver came to St. John's to study at Memorial University, and stayed. He is a Newfoundlander and Labradorian by choice. He was asking similar questions, having similar conversations.

We embarked on an examination of the history of Black people in early Newfoundland and Labrador and of how their legacy remains with us today. We hope this book inspires others to dive in and ask questions of their own.

Who Was W.H.?
HB

We started our quest to find out more by digging into the recent past: June 1987.

L'Anse au Loup, a small fishing community on the south coast of Labrador, is a quiet spot. Most people who live there enjoy a low-key life, connected to work on the sea. Across the Strait of Belle Isle, the twinkling lights of communities on Newfoundland's Northern Peninsula are visible.

L'Anse au Loup is a French name—early visitors might have named the place after wolves, or maybe *loup marins*—seals. Seals, cod, and whales would have drawn the French to this remote section of the North Atlantic coastline. They were not the only Europeans to land in the area—they would have run into Spanish and British sailors as well. But it was not just Europeans who chanced upon L'Anse au Loup over the past few hundred years.

In June 1987, a local resident went for a walk in the community and made a grim discovery. Just outside the town cemetery, bones, wood, and textiles were jutting out of a sandy bank. Human remains. Memorial University archaeologist Dr. James Tuck and his team from St. John's were called to investigate.

Once in L'Anse au Loup, the team found something even more startling. In that sandy bank, they found a wooden coffin with the unusually well-preserved remains of a young Black man, wrapped in a woollen blanket, with his woollen naval uniform laid on the blanket. Along with the uniform, a few belongings were in the coffin—leather shoes, buttons, and a knife handle carved with *W.H.* Based on their excavations and investigations, the team concluded that W.H. was in his 20s when he died. He had likely been a crew member aboard a ship off the south coast of Labrador. His death was unexpected, and he was buried in L'Anse au Loup, sometime in the early 1800s.

The team still had more questions than answers. What was a young Black man doing there in the early 1800s? Where was he originally from? Why was he not buried at sea?

In 1987, most people in Newfoundland and Labrador would not have considered that, in past centuries, a Black man, free or enslaved, would have been anywhere near our shores. Did Black people not live in the United States or the Caribbean? Were these not the places where the terrible history of slavery happened?

Why, then, was W.H.'s final resting place the northerly community of L'Anse au Loup? Why was the man buried in such a specific way, in a wooden coffin with personal belongings? How did he die? How did he live?

Who was W.H.?

Details about the discovery were presented in a 1995 article published in the *Canadian Journal of Archaeology*.[2] Hardly anyone outside of archaeological circles took notice of it. The story, and mystery, of W.H. remained buried to the world at large, until 2020.

That year, W.H.'s uniform went on display at The Rooms, Newfoundland and Labrador's modern glass and steel art gallery, museum, and archives complex in the provincial capital city of

---

2   Cathy Mathias and Sonja M. Jerkic, "Investigating W.H.: A Nineteenth Century Burial from L'Anse Au Loup, Labrador," *Canadian Journal of Archaeology* 19 (1995): 101-16, https://www.jstor.org/stable/41102572.

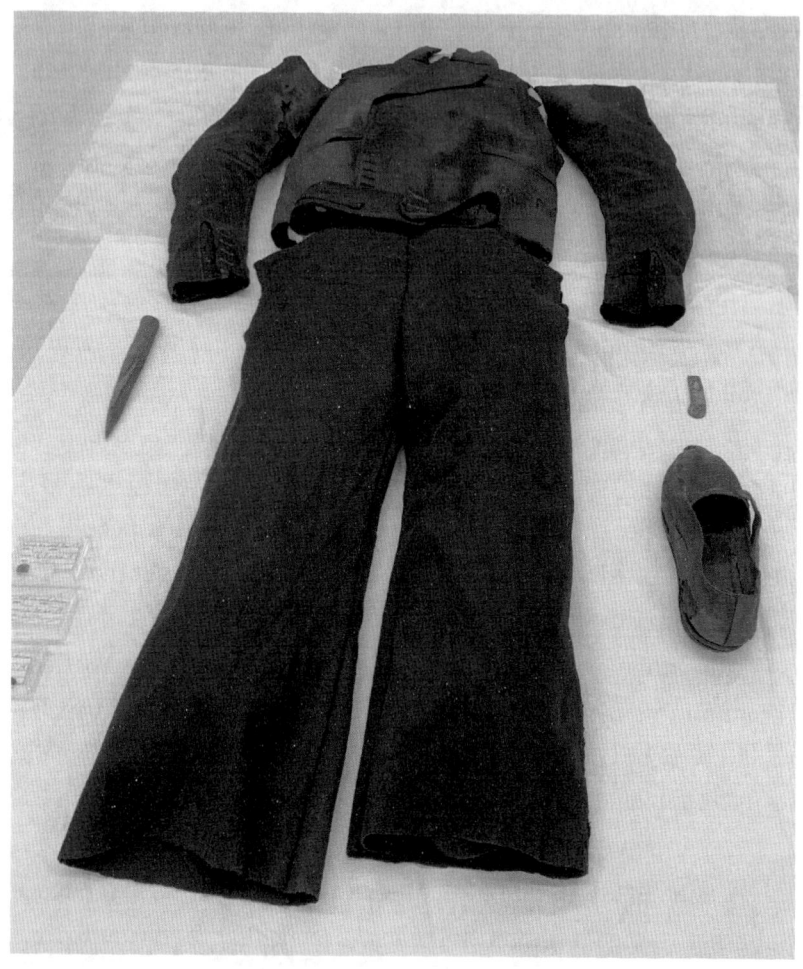

The uniform and objects found buried with W.H. in L'Anse au Loup, Labrador, now stored at The Rooms in St. John's. *Heather Barrett*

St. John's. It was part of the exhibit "What Carries Us: Newfoundland and Labrador in the Black Atlantic" curated by Bushra Junaid, an artist, curator, and Black Canadian who grew up in St. John's.

As of 2023, W.H.'s remains and his belongings are stored far away from public view, in a climate-controlled purpose-built basement area of The Rooms, in the Archaeology and Indigenous Peoples' collection.

We had an opportunity to visit that room, in a section of The Rooms that is closed to the public. We descended a staircase and entered an area located behind heavy, double blue doors.

Laid out carefully on a table were a pair of navy blue woollen pants, a dark vest and jacket, and a single leather shoe. W.H.'s belongings. The clothing was in good shape; it looked well enough preserved that a small person today could crawl into them. On the table, laid next to the clothing, were a few small copper buttons, a leather knife sheath, and the wooden handle of a knife, carved clearly with *W.H.*

As for W.H., his remains are stored in that room according to proper archaeological standards, out of sight. W.H.'s remains need to be claimed by kin; and then the government of Newfoundland and Labrador can release them for burial. So far, no one and no group have claimed kinship of W.H.

Who *was* W.H.?

Was he the only Black person working—and dying—in Newfoundland and Labrador at that time? Were there more? Were W.H. and/or others enslaved, as were most Black people in the New World at that time? Why have we not heard more about any of this?

The Almighty Cod
HB

The reason that W.H., and everyone else, came to Newfoundland and the coast of Labrador over the centuries can be hooked into one small, powerful word: cod. It is a word—and a food—that is still on the tip of the tongue in Newfoundland and Labrador. In cod we trust.

Back to the 1490s, though, and eastward across the Atlantic. At that time, Europe was in an age of innovation, exploration, and discovery. New technologies in navigation and shipbuilding permitted voyagers to travel farther across the oceans. The monarchies in Spain, Portugal, and England sent crews and their ships in all directions, looking for riches to bring back to their own countries: gold, spices, tea.

European explorers speculated that by heading westward across the Atlantic, they would discover new sea routes to the Orient, now called Asia. That would make it easier to transport goods from there back to Europe. The race was on to see which European country would reach which far-flung land first, to claim those lands and their riches for their own.

Explorers made landfall in places that we now know are in the Caribbean and along the east coasts of North and South America. For the Europeans, this was the Age of Discovery; for the Indigenous peoples who had lived there for thousands of years, it became an age of disruption and, often, death.

Italian navigator and explorer Giovanni Caboto, known in English as John Cabot, dreamed of the glory that his fellow Italian explorer Christopher Columbus had received on his triumphant return from his discovery of the New World of the Americas in 1492. Caboto had been based in England for two years, waiting to be sent westward by King Henry VII. In 1497, Caboto's time came. He took a more northward route across the Atlantic Ocean, and landed his small ship, the *Matthew*, somewhere on the east coast of the island of Newfoundland, possibly at Bonavista.

Caboto did not find a route to the Orient, or the fruitful bounty of the Caribbean Islands, but he found something better: the Atlantic cod. The Atlantic cod is a large, predatory fish, roughly 30 centimetres to 1 metre long. It is a bottom feeder, eating whatever it can find close to the ocean floor.

Newfoundland and the northeastern part of North America border on relatively shallow parts of the Atlantic Ocean, which were hospitable environments for cod. On these banks, the warm Gulf Stream and the cold Labrador Current meet, creating conditions in which cod thrive. The Grand Banks, the most densely populated area of this underwater continental shelf, was home to millions and millions of cod.

In Caboto's day, the waters around Newfoundland were the most productive fishing grounds Europeans had ever encountered. Correspondence related to Caboto's voyage describes sailors lowering baskets over the side of the *Matthew* and pulling them up laden with cod.

The *Matthew*'s crew had important news to report to the king of England. Western Europeans consumed cod in large quantities. Many European countries had "fish days," when eating meat was illegal for religious reasons. Not only was cod in high demand but it was also an early superfood. Cod was plentiful and tasty and a high source of protein. Its delicate white flesh was prized. Almost every part of the cod was edible. Most European countries had their own favourite parts and their own special cod recipes. Cod was easily preserved, salted or dried, for long distances across the Atlantic Ocean.

In French, cod is *morue*; in Spanish, *bacalao*; in Portuguese, *bacalhau*. To this day, in Newfoundland, cod is simply called *fish*, because that was almost all the fish there was.

Word of this bounty quickly spread. In the early 1500s, Portuguese and Spanish ships explored and fished off the coast of Newfoundland. By the mid-1500s, English and French vessels followed them. The marks of these countries and their early explorations are still found on Newfoundland and Labrador maps. Place names such as Cape Spear and Fogo Island come from the Portuguese. The fishing communities of Spanish Room and Port aux Basques were named by the Spanish. Bay d'Espoir and Placentia, among others, are French names.

By the end of the 1500s, cod was an in-demand food and also a commodity.[3] England traded cod from Newfoundland with France, Spain, Portugal, and Italy for other goods. Cod was gold—and Newfoundland and its ports the site of the rush. Europeans with power and seeking more power came here.

Anyone and everyone passed through Newfoundland's ports.

---

[3] George A. Rose, *Cod: The Ecological History of the North Atlantic Fisheries* (Breakwater Books, Ltd., 2007), 67.

Enslavement and the Triangular Trade
HB

By the early 1500s, cod from the waters surrounding Newfoundland was in high demand in Europe. This made the island of Newfoundland and the south coast of Labrador strategic locations in the Atlantic Ocean.

To put this in perspective, we follow the cod. We have to look at what was happening at that time in the other nations whose shorelines bordered the Atlantic Ocean. Portugal, Spain, Britain, and France—the countries which sent ships to fish Newfoundland waters, landed in Newfoundland ports, and, in France and England's case, established colonies—were among the most successful European colonizers.

The establishment of colonies was a way for these prosperous, white countries to claim ownership of lands and resources in the New World. They planted their flags anywhere their ships could sail: Asia, North and South America, and Africa.

Establishing colonies was dangerous work. The voyage across the treacherous North Atlantic, in small wooden ships, with close, unsanitary quarters, was hazardous. Disease and accidents were part of life at sea. Ships often sank. Many of those who boarded ships in Europe died before they reached the New World.

For those who survived, clearing land, growing crops, building houses and buildings, and fishing were backbreaking tasks. Living conditions were rough—very basic food and shelter, and little to help those who became ill or were injured. Then there were conflicts, with Indigenous people who found their lands and waterways stolen from them by the incoming Europeans, and wars between European countries to determine who "owned" these new lands.

All this required human workers and labour, more than the colonizing countries' populations could provide. It is no wonder that our history books are filled with tales of poor and desperate people who took a chance on voyaging to the New World—if you were not poor or desperate, why would you sign up for this?

Colonization had a massive human resources problem. Where would the colonizers find enough people to do this dangerous work? European colonizers looked to Africa for a solution. Along with gold and spices, Africa had another resource: people. Humans with Black skin. Humans who did not look like Europeans. Enslaved Black Africans were the answer.

Starting in the 1500s and lasting for more than 300 years, European colonizers captured and enslaved about 12.8 million African people for unpaid labour in the New World.

It was the European business model, the terrible cost of expansion. Portugal, Spain, Britain, France, and the Netherlands were the European nations trading in the largest numbers of enslaved people. Slavery and the trade and loss of souls were written into their countries' laws. It was legal to not consider Black Africans to be people. They were chattel. Enslavement became a key part of an Atlantic-wide system known as the triangular trade.

Europeans sailed south on the Atlantic Ocean to the coast of Africa with manufactured goods for trade—rum, sugar, cotton—which they had brought back across the Atlantic from the West Indies. Other manufactured goods, such as muskets, bullets, and guns, were used for what was about to happen in Africa.

Those goods were traded and used to enforce the trade for humans: Black Africans.

Along with gold and spices, humans were just another cargo that Europeans took from Africa. Enslaved Africans were crammed by the hundreds into ships, below decks, shackled, and taken eastward across the Atlantic. This part of the slave trade, the transport of Black human cargo across the Atlantic to the Americas, was known as the Middle Passage.

Historians estimate that at least 2 million Africans died on the Middle Passage. They died when ships sank. They died from the conditions they suffered while crammed into the windowless hulls of ships. Some were tortured and murdered by their captors.

Once the ships and their human cargo reached land in the Americas, Black Africans were then resold or traded. Enslaved Black people were exploited and abused at farms, fields, and mines, as domestic servants, and at sea. Slave labour produced goods from the riches of the New World, which were shipped eastward, back across the Atlantic, to be consumed in Europe.

Most of these millions of enslaved Black Africans were taken to South America and the Caribbean. About 10 per cent of them were brought to North America, mostly to what is now the United States. A few came north, to places that eventually became Canada. Generations upon generations of Black people were born into slavery. This complex system of economic expansion based upon human oppression lasted from about 1500 to the mid-1800s.

Newfoundland and Labrador had its own corner in the triangular trade. Again, we follow the cod. Salted cod, fished and prepared in Newfoundland, was sent on ships heading back to Europe and on ships heading south to the Caribbean.

"The ships would go down to the southern portion of the Americas, especially the West Indian islands there," says Dr. Afua Cooper, an historian at Dalhousie University, an author, and a poet. Cooper is a Black woman with a deep interest in the history and experiences of Black people in eastern Canada. In an interview, she explains the triangular trade: "They [Newfoundland-based businesspeople] would exchange the dried fish, salted pork, salted beef, flour, with the plantation owners who would then send up the tropical items." Salted cod from Newfoundland, and the early days of the other Atlantic provinces, became a staple food in Jamaica. In fact, Newfoundland had a type of codfish, a dried cod called Jamaica grade: "The better grades, the better cuts, were sent to Europe and the Mediterranean, and the worst cod came to the islands."

That information, salted and dried in lower-grade cod from Newfoundland, tells a darker story about early Newfoundland and Labrador, and who, exactly, helped feed the demand for fish from that area of the North Atlantic.

"You didn't have to go over to Africa or go over to Europe," Cooper says. "You could stay right in Newfoundland, which, oftentimes, is what happened."

Xaiver Chats Cod
XMC

In Jamaica, it is said that if you ever saw the head of the salt fish, you would neva nyam e, cause e fava wa mansta. The head was evil and full of crosses.[4] These were my first lessons about salt fish.

By the age of 10, I started shadowing my grandmother in our kitchen. I observed the care that went into preparing our national dish, ackee and salt fish. First Grandma dropped the whole flattened filet of fish into a bowl of water while we prepared the ackee. Ackee demands careful attention, since it can be poisonous. On Sunday mornings, when akee was in season, we would pick the bright red and yellowish ackee pods from the tree. Grandma taught me to pick only the ackees that had opened on their own, as a closed ackee or one that is forced open is potentially lethal. The firm, pale yellow fruit was then plucked from its pod. It was my job to pinch off the large black seed atop the fruit. Next Grandma removed the pink vein in the middle of the ackee. Eating this pink tissue is also potentially fatal. The cleaned ackee was put aside to wait for its companion, the soaking salt fish. Grandma retrieved the long strip of soaking fish and diligently picked out all the bones. We both then ripped the salt fish into smaller pieces. Grandma then resubmerged the fish to rehydrate and rid it of any extra salt.

---

4   Robert Lalah, "Codfish Fears Conquered," *The Jamaica Gleaner*, May 19, 2009, http://old.jamaica-gleaner.com/gleaner/20090519/life/life1.html.

When I was allowed to start going to the shop by myself, it always excited me to see "one pound of salt fish" on the grocery list. I peered into the brown paper the fish was wrapped in with hopes of laying eyes on the head. Part of me knew I was the only Jamaican that could see the head of the salt fish and still eat it in any dish presented to me. After countless trips to the shop, I still had not seen the salt-fish head, and it was not for a lack of trying. I assumed the salt fish came to the shop without its mysterious, monstrous head.

Salt fish, salt cod, codfish. Monster. It goes by many names.

The Jamaican salt fish I am used to is paper thin. One side is silver and spotted, the cod's skin, and the flesh side an off-white, sometimes yellowish, colour. Best practice was to soak the fish for 8 hours, or overnight if you could. If not, the fish could be boiled to rid it of most of its saltiness. The crucial takeaway from cooking ackee and salt fish is that no excess salt was required. Into the pot went a little oil, chopped onions, pimento seeds, Scotch bonnet, and crushed garlic. I eagerly observed everything my grandmother did as if she were a flowing well and me an insatiable sponge. As the onions sizzled in the dutchie, the large grey pot on the other burner bubbled. Filled with food or ground provisions dug from a nearby field, the rolling pieces of yam, Irish potato, dasheen, and plantains all vied for time on the surface. I smiled at the three fingers of green banana still whole in the pot, my favourite.

When the salt fish was hydrated, it still did not look like any fish I had ever seen. It did not flake like the snapper, or the butterfish pulled from the Caribbean Sea. Grandma pulled the pieces of papery fish from its soaking bowl and stirred them into the pot with the onions. After minutes of simmering, in went the bright yellow pieces of ackee. Great care was taken to not break up the ackee too much or, worse, overcook it. Ackee was supposed to be firm in the mouth yet tender, not anything close to the texture of mashed potatoes.

When ackee was not in season, the salt fish found itself in fried dough known as stamp and go, or cooked down with beans, onions, and coconut milk in a dish called run dung.

Newfoundland codfish had been swimming through my veins long before I first landed at St. John's International Airport. But now that I live in Newfoundland and Labrador, I can eat fresh cod. My tastebuds have developed an affinity for codfish that did not require rehydration. Steamed with garlic or pan-fried in olive oil are my preferred ways to consume cod, but I love fish and brewis, fish cakes, and deep-fried tongues. The options feel endless.

The Atlantic Ocean separates me physically from Jamaica but houses the fish that stirs immense feelings of home. So much that I can comfortably call this new place, Newfoundland and Labrador, home.

I called my mother and asked her about the lore of the monstrous cod head. She told me that we only ever got the thin fish in Jamaica. I remembered the sheets of paper that passed for fish. I thought about the disconnect that Jamaicans, me included, have from this fish that has become synonymous with Jamaican food culture.

How could this mysterious fish be cemented into the lives of so many people? There must have been one person who had glimpsed the cod head. As a child, I mulled over the secrets of the almighty cod. It has been decades since I was that child in our family kitchen in Jamaica watching my grandmother cook. Now I am a writer, and because Newfoundland and Jamaica are the two places I am most familiar with, my writing centres on both islands.

Cod first made its way to Jamaica in the 16th century, during the transatlantic slave trade. As Gina Snooks and Sonja Boon state, salt fish, "a key product of Newfoundland's outport local economies and central to understandings of gendered bodily labour—became a staple element of West Indian slave and Creole diets."[5] That same thin, papery fish flooded my childhood food memories of joyous meals with family.

I have now come face to face with the same codfish multiple times. Once was during a screech-in at Memorial University. Another time, during a turbulent cod-jigging excursion which left me a few pounds lighter from seasickness but with half a dozen spotted Atlantic cod.

Both these times I looked for the monster in the face of the fish. One fish had the beginnings of a beard but that was nothing to fear. The beard was more reminiscent of that stray hair that forms on your great-auntie's chin and not that of a lumberjack.

I wonder if it is time that Newfoundlanders and Labradorians take a closer look at their history. The monster lurking may be difficult to face but nothing to fear. The disconnect between the lived realities of those enslaved in the Caribbean and the early settlers of Newfoundland has allowed such monsters, myths, and misinformation to prevail. Newfoundland Black history is not well known, yet Black struggle and workmanship are engrained in Newfoundland culture.

"A fully bearded fish is something to fear, but not the head of the cod." I told my mother they cut the head off before the fish is salted, well before it trickles down to Jamaican hands. With pleasure, I dispelled the myth of the cod head.

---

5   Gina Snooks and Sonja Boon, "Salt Fish and Molasses: Unsettling the Palate in the Spaces between Two Continents," *The European Journal of Life Writing* 6 (2017): 218-41, quotation at 219, https://ejlw.eu/article/view/31492/28851.

Heather Goes to Lagos
HB

Portugal and Newfoundland have been deeply connected over the centuries, bound by a history of seafaring, of Portuguese fishing fleets visiting Newfoundland ports, by cod. Portugal, a small European country bordering the eastern edge of the Atlantic Ocean, has a deep and impressive maritime history.

Portugal is also home to the southwestern port town of Lagos, a place which can be pinpointed as ground zero of the transatlantic slave trade.

In the 1400s, Portugal became the world's leading maritime power. Portugal's Prince Henry, known as "the Navigator," established a naval college in the Algarve, the southern region of Portugal, where Lagos is located. The Algarve, a hotbed of innovation, attracted a multicultural group of specialists from nearby ocean-bordering lands: north Africa, the Mediterranean, and Europe. Map-makers, shipbuilders, scientists, and inventors. Southern Portugal was a 15th-century, maritime version of Silicon Valley.

The Portuguese developed the navigation and shipbuilding technology that enabled explorers to venture farther across the oceans than ever before. Portugal became a country of exploration, colonization, and trade, going to far-flung lands—the Americas, including Newfoundland, southeast Asia, and Africa.

In 1444, a ship docked in Lagos. It carried 235 Black Africans, who were taken to a piece of land just outside the town walls and sold at an open-air market. The largest-scale human trafficking event in the world had begun: the transatlantic slave trade.

By 1600, the Portuguese practice of using enslaved Black people as unpaid and exploitable workers had spread through all the European colonizing countries. Spain, England, France, and the Netherlands all solved their never-ending demand for labour in the New World by enslaving Black people.

Between 1444 and the 1860s, when slavery ended, at least 15 million Africans were removed from their continent.[6] Generations of Black people were born to enslaved parents, and those babies automatically became the property of white owners.

Today, Portugal, the country which started the transatlantic slave trade, is a peaceful country of about 10 million people and a popular tourist destination. Its people are relaxed and friendly, its scenery beautiful, its culture vibrant. *Bacalhau*, which translates in English as salt cod, is on every restaurant menu. I had the good fortune to spend a few months in Portugal in the spring of 2022. I immediately felt the connections between this southern European country and Newfoundland and Labrador.

The Portuguese are proud of their history of maritime exploration and innovation. Museums and monuments throughout the nation are dedicated to telling the stories of navigation, shipbuilding, and the brave explorers who ventured forth on the seas. But the Portuguese do not talk much about their role in an important part of the Age of Discovery—the transatlantic slave trade.

The Mercado de Escravos, the Slave Market, in Lagos is the only museum in Portugal devoted to telling the story of the enslavement of Black African people and the start of the centuries-

---

6   Afua Cooper, *The Hanging of Angelique: The Untold Story of Canadian Slavery and the Burning of Old Montreal* (HarperCollins, 2006).

long transatlantic slave trade. The museum is part of the UNESCO Slave Route Project, an initiative designed to help break the silence around the history of slavery.

Even in the low tourist season, Lagos is popular with European and North American visitors; nearly all of them are white, like me. It is home to about 31,000 people, and its large marina is filled with well-maintained sailboats and small yachts. Small, white, stucco hotels dot the harbourfront. An attractive boardwalk has kiosks advertising boat tours and fishing expeditions. You can rent sea kayaks and paddle boards on cliff-lined sandy beaches. You can dine on octopus and drink vinho verde. You can party the night away at one of Lagos's glamorous nightclubs. A holiday paradise.

I walked from the train station, around the marina, and down the long, festive boardwalk to the old section of Lagos, near the end of its harbour, closer to the Atlantic Ocean. There, I found myself in a large public square. To one side were the remnants of ancient Moorish city walls and an old fort. On another side of the square was a large Roman Catholic church. Directly across from that church was a small, two-storey, white stucco building. The Mercado de Escravos. I walked across the square, paid the museum entrance fee, and entered a part of history which had not been taught in the classrooms of my childhood.

Inside, on the first floor, was a small room, painted white and dotted with floor-to-ceiling black pillars. Each pillar held information—maps of the town of Lagos, maps of the transatlantic slave route, text explaining the history of enslaved Black people in the area. A straw sculpture in the middle of the room was an abstract representation of one of the Black enslaved people in Lagos. The exhibit continued on a second floor: more black pillars, more maps and text, a few historical illustrations of Lagos from the era.

But where were all the Black people? The exhibit had a few illustrated depictions of enslaved Africans, fully clothed, walking around old Lagos carrying baskets on their heads or attending the Church of St. Sebastien, a Catholic church set up for the Africans outside the town walls. In text, the museum described how slaves were sorted according to colour and size, to their great distress, and to the "amazement" of local townspeople. A photograph of a skeleton, unearthed at the site of the town's old dump, shows where the bodies of Black Africans were flung.

Flung there along with other bits of 14th-century rubbish. Although the museum's information booklet informs the reader, "it is important to note that even in the context of the same rubbish tip, some bones have been found which suggest that the bodies were carefully placed there, perhaps by other slaves who were friends or relatives."

I ask the museum attendant if many people in Portugal knew much about their country's role in the transatlantic slave trade. She says they did not. I also wondered about the name Lagos. Was that where Lagos, Nigeria, the massive urban sprawl of 23 million people, the largest city in Africa, got its name? "Yes," the museum interpreter confirms. "The Portuguese explorers named that place Lagos because the land reminded them of *their* Lagos."

Here I was, in one of the most significant ports of the Black Atlantic, and the more I learned, the more questions I had: What about the large numbers of slaves that flowed through Lagos and the rest of Portugal for centuries? What about the horrors that Black Africans endured at the hands of their Portuguese and other European captors? What about the dangerous and backbreaking work enslaved Africans did against their will to build European riches? What about their deaths in captivity?

I began to feel nauseous. It was too much to take in. I needed air. Unlike the millions of Black African slaves in the hulls of ships, I had the liberty of finding the door and getting out.

I exited the Mercado de Escravos, walked across the square, and crossed the street to a small strip of sandy beach, bordered on one side by rocky cliffs. I stepped around the boats and equipment for a small sailing school and walked out along the breakwater to the open ocean.

I have walked out on many breakwaters on the other side of the Atlantic, at home in Newfoundland. Here in Lagos, my view of the open ocean was roughly southward, so the next point of land, invisible on the horizon, was somewhere on the west coast of Africa. Even though I could not see Africa on the horizon, Portugal is so close to that continent that reddish-brown sand from Sahara dust storms regularly coats Portuguese cars and patio furniture.

I stared out at the ocean and listened to the waves wash up on the beach behind me. I took a deep breath of salty sea air. It smelled so familiar. Like Newfoundland. Like home.

I wondered about the Africans who were captured, brought across the ocean, and somehow wound up in Newfoundland, hundreds of years ago. Did the ocean look, smell, and sound like home to them, too? Where, exactly, did they come from? Were they enslaved, working in terrible conditions, in places where there was salty air? The roar of the waves? Or did the Atlantic Ocean become their grave?

Black Sailors
HB

"I feel like the world is more infinitely interesting than we think," says Camille Turner. "There was a lot of movement in the age of sail. There were three times as many Africans crossing the Atlantic as there were Europeans." Turner, an artist and academic based in Toronto, has been discovering *who else* came to Newfoundland and Labrador, those who most historians may not have noticed.

In 2019, Turner brought her multimedia project, the *Afronautic Research Lab*, to the Bonavista Biennale, a rural, public art event on Newfoundland's Bonavista Peninsula. Her project invited visitors to think about historical links between Newfoundland and Labrador and the transatlantic slave trade. Turner has done much work on this herself.

Swimming in the same ocean of research as Turner is Dr. Neil Kennedy, an associate professor of Caribbean history at Memorial University. "The English wanted to emulate the Spanish and one element of Spanish success in the Americas was associated with slavery," he says. "And so, in modelling themselves on early Spanish success, the English adopted slavery."

One thing that made Black Africans, especially those who came from coastal areas, especially useful to the English, explains Kennedy, is they were known to be exceptionally good at working on the ocean: "West Africans were some of the most skilled boatmen and small boatmen and were employed in those tasks throughout the Caribbean and in places with coastal rivers like North Carolina, South Carolina, Georgia." Many Black Africans were excellent sailors and fishers—workers who would have been in high demand in the fishery off the coast of Newfoundland. "Africans were very highly represented in the coastal trades for their skill."

West Africans fished, traded, and fought from canoes on the ocean and rivers.[7] They also felt a deep cultural and spiritual connection to water.

Others, through the horror of the Middle Passage, became acquainted with the skills needed for survival during long periods at sea. These skills were exploited by the Europeans who owned them, and many enslaved people wound up in dangerous work at sea, on fishing boats, doing transport work, or on naval vessels. Enslaved Black people who were brought to the Caribbean and coastal areas of the Americas continued doing water-based work for generations. In warmer waters, they were excellent divers, swimmers, and canoeists.

Even in modern times, working at sea is considered a dangerous way to make a living. Both Kennedy and Turner note that going to sea in the 16th, 17th, and 18th centuries was even more hazardous, and frequently deadly.

"They [Europeans] used up sailors like nobody's business," Turner says. "In any kind of profession, that's dangerous. That's difficult, that there is a shortage. That's where people on the bottom of the social scale are going to get employment."

The people at the bottom of this social scale were Black.

In the harsh, close confines of a ship at sea, living conditions were poor for everyone, and the environment—a small ship exposed in the rough waters of the Atlantic—was dangerous.[8] Everyone had to work together to survive.

---

7   W. Jeffrey Bolster, *Black Jacks: African American Seamen in the Age of Sail* (Harvard University Press, 1997), 62.
8   Bolster, *Black Jacks*, 102.

In these squalid conditions, life might have been slightly better for enslaved Black people at sea than those on land. Black and white crew members worked side by side in a more equal environment than anywhere on land. Black men, through their skills, occasionally rose to officer ranks on vessels. Sometimes, Black sailors even wore uniforms. Like that worn by W.H. Sometimes, for Black sailors, the line between enslaved and free was blurred. "We know by the 18th century, about one-fifth of all sailors in the Atlantic, in the Merchant Marine were people of colour, both free and enslaved, and about the same percentage, about one-fifth of the Royal Navy sailors were people of colour as well by the end of the 18th century," Kennedy says.

One out of every five sailors aboard British vessels in the 18th century was a person of colour. Other European countries, emulating the highly successful British Navy, could not have been far behind.

During these same centuries, interest in the fisheries in the waters off Newfoundland and Labrador was booming. Ships from Portugal, Spain, England, France, and the Caribbean were coming to the waters all around this corner of the North Atlantic to fish for cod. Does that mean that Black sailors, enslaved or free, would have been on ships that docked in Newfoundland harbours and ports?

Kennedy found passing mentions of calculations concerning cargo while digging through port records in England and the Caribbean from the 1600s. Some of these calculations involve people. He found a reference in an old port book from a record keeper in Southampton, England: "He [the record keeper] notes that in 1626, that on his way from Southampton to Virginia, he stops in Newfoundland, and purchases 80,000 fish and a slave. Now that individual story we know nothing about. And that slave ended up presumably sold in Virginia as well, along with that load of fish. But how that individual was here in the first place, we simply don't know."

Knowing that crews aboard ships were multi-ethnic, and knowing that slavery was ubiquitous in European seafaring countries, it is likely that both enslaved and free Black people would have been aboard ships that fished Newfoundland waters and docked in Newfoundland ports. "It is also likely that, as in that 1626 record, enslaved Black people were purchased and traded along the way," Kennedy points out. "Whether that would be between the ships of various nations that spent time in Newfoundland ports, or on land, is still to be determined."

More research is needed to pinpoint exact names, dates, and places. Black people who were enslaved were not often logged by name. By law, they were not people, but property. Researchers are beginning to connect the dots by looking at adjacent evidence, such as burials. "The Royal Navy Cemetery in St. John's, when it was excavated, included the remains of a number of people of colour," Kennedy adds.

And what about W.H., buried farther north, on the south coast of Labrador? Could he have been a crew member aboard a ship from Bermuda, or a member of the British Royal Navy?

As Kennedy says, "He [W.H.] is one of many people that we simply don't know enough about."

Black Slavery in Canada
HB

"Newfoundland has always been in my consciousness," Afua Cooper tells us. "With regards to our [Jamaican] cuisine and how the codfish is such an important part of it. In fact, Newfoundland had a type of codfish, dried cod called Jamaica grade, which wasn't the best grade." Cooper writes in *The Hanging of Angelique* that "Canada was not a slave society—that is, a society whose economy was based on slavery—but it was a society with slaves."[9]

In North America, we tend to think of slavery as operating on an industrial farming scale—that is, a huge cotton, tobacco, or sugar cane plantation, with each plantation worked by hand by hundreds of slaves, in brutal conditions, often for a cruel master. Poverty, disease, and violence were part of their daily existence. And that is how it mostly worked in the southern United States and the Caribbean; their economies were fuelled by the enslaved labour of millions of Africans and their descendants.

What would life have been like for enslaved people connected to Newfoundland from the 1500s to the 1800s? No farming plantations existed in Newfoundland. Large-scale agriculture was not feasible as the weather was too cold and harsh, and the rocky terrain was unsuitable. On the east coast of the island, early settlers barely had enough topsoil to grow a few root vegetables for their own consumption.

---

9 Cooper, *The Hanging of Angelique*, 68.

For clues, we can turn to what life was like for enslaved people in northeastern North America, in what eventually became the Canadian province of Quebec, and the Maritime provinces of New Brunswick, Nova Scotia, and Prince Edward Island. There were no plantations in those areas, either. But much hard labour needed to be done, and there were not enough Europeans to do it.

"A useful definition of slavery is the robbery of one's freedom and labour by another, usually more powerful person," Cooper writes. "Violence and coercion are used to carry out the theft and to keep the slave captive in the condition of bondage and servitude. This definition applies to slavery in Canada."[10]

According to Cooper's research, European colonists first tried to enslave the Indigenous people they encountered in northeastern North America. But many Indigenous people died as a result of the harsh conditions of slavery. They also died from diseases introduced by the Europeans and from the violence dealt from the hands of Europeans.

Black slaves did not die as quickly as the Indigenous people. Therefore, Cooper says, European colonizers had the notion that Black people were stronger and better suited to enslaved labour. Colonizers would have been familiar with the use of enslaved Black people in Europe and other parts of the New World, so why not use them farther north? For centuries, treating enslaved Black people as tools for free, dangerous labour was simply the way Europeans did business.

From 1628 to 1833, laws by both French and English colonists in early Canada made slavery legal, and holding enslaved people was common practice by both French and English colonists.

"There were laws that said Black people were commodities," Cooper says. "They could be bought, sold, and traded across colonial

---

10   Cooper, *The Hanging of Angelique*, 70.

imperial frontiers. In laws in all of the colonial empires, including the British Empire, it was sanctioned—the murder of Black people. A slave could be killed for no reason. Maimed, dismembered, castrated. Slave women didn't own the children that they gave birth to."

Enslaved Black people in Quebec and the Maritimes did coerced labour, whatever was needed to support the fur trade in Quebec: house servants, rat catchers, small-scale farmers, and tradespeople.

"In Maritime areas like the Atlantic colonies [provinces] and New England, you had many slave masters who used their slaves as fishermen," says Cooper. "Fishing is big. And so, for me, if there's a clue that you want to follow in studying Atlantic Black history, look at the fishing trade, look at the maritime occupations."

What does this have to do with Newfoundland and Labrador? Newfoundland was not even part of Canada until the second half of the 20th century. Until that time, it was its own country, Britain's oldest colony, until 1949, when it joined Canada.

Consider, Cooper suggests, the first recorded sale of a Black African in Canada, in Quebec in 1628. A nine-year-old boy from Madagascar was sold by British colonist David Kirke to a Quebec clerk. That boy was then sold a second time, and in 1633, was baptized with the French name Olivier Le Jeune.[11] Several years later, Kirke, now Sir David Kirke, a known slave owner, turned up in Newfoundland, at the Colony of Avalon. This is a key moment for Black Harbour.

Some enslaved people in early Canada tried to escape, as they did elsewhere. Cooper has scoured centuries-old newspapers and public documents from maritime companies in early Canada for clues of their flights and has found advertisements from these companies seeking information about escaped slaves: "There is this tantalizing

---

11   Cooper, *The Hanging of Angelique*, 70.

phrase [in those ads] that says, 'he may take off on a boat bound for Newfoundland.' So, there's always that possibility if ships are leaving port in Saint John, New Brunswick or Halifax, Nova Scotia, some of them are going to Newfoundland."

Cooper has read the archaeological account of the discovery of W.H.'s remains on the south coast of Labrador, and she, too, has spent considerable time thinking about this Black man and how his final resting place became the sandy shore of a fishing community, likely thousands of miles from his birthplace. She concludes, "This is perhaps the metaphor for Black history in Newfoundland. For 200 years, this man lay there sleeping. And then one day, he decided to rise up."

Xaymaca and Spanish Conquest
XMC

The First People in Newfoundland saw their way of life changed forever after colonizers arrived, and similar tremors of change were felt farther south in Xaymaca.

The First People of Xaymaca arrived on that tiny Caribbean island 2,500 years ago. They were the Arawakan-speaking Taino people. Peaceful and industrious, they grew cassava, sweet potatoes, fruits, and cotton. Tobacco was farmed widely; smoking was a common amusement. The Taino lived across Xaymaca, but many stayed by the coast and rivers, and fish was a crucial ingredient in their diets. Xaymaca was their land of wood and water. These people led quiet lives until their encounters with Europeans.

On his second voyage to the West Indies, in 1494 Columbus arrived in St. Ann's Bay, on the north coast of Xaymaca, considered by the Cubans as the land of blessed gold. There was no gold to be found in Jamaica. The Taino attacked the Spanish ships to protect their land from invasion. Determined to annex the island for the Spain, Columbus persisted. While at Discovery Bay, a town farther down the coast, he was met again by hostility from the Taino. Columbus's men overthrew the Taino, claiming the land and killing many of them in the process.

After the Spanish settled on Xaymaca, they enslaved and brutalized the Taino. Spanish settlers brought diseases the Indigenous people had no immunity against, leading to more deaths. Academic literature has repeatedly reproduced the misconception about the extinction of Xaymaca's Indigenous Taino population.

Continued colonial narratives of complete Indigenous decimation in the Caribbean enforce this enduring myth.

Others argue that the Indigenous Taino people of Xaymaca survived and, along with escaped enslaved Africans, were the original ancestors of some Maroons on the island and resistors to enslavement. Since Taino people were assumed annihilated before Maroon communities formed, popular history considers Maroons on the island to be the descendants of escaped enslaved Africans, enabling a separation of Xaymaca's Taino and African histories. A 2018 DNA-based study of Accompong Town Maroons[12] of connects both histories, offering genetic evidence suggesting Indigenous Americans, possibly the Taino, occupied Xaymaca's hinterlands before and after the 1655 British invasion, and that interactions between the African Maroons and the Taino were likely. Further, they posit that some present day Accompong Town Maroon genetic ancestry extends beyond Africa to include Indigenous Americans, possibly the Taino. While more research is needed to determine if the Taino were the first Maroons, this study strengthens the claim of present-day Taino survival among Maroons.

In 1509, the first established European settlement of the island, Sevilla la Nueva, was created. Jamaica, a bastardization of Xaymaca, appears on maps of the New World. Spanish colonial development of Xaymaca stagnated. The island was mainly used as a supply base for Spain's continued conquest of the Americas. The first enslaved Africans were brought to Jamaica in 1513 from the Iberian Peninsula. Piracy thrived alongside early Spanish settlements; these buccaneers were a bastion of the fleeting masterless class in the Caribbean and Xaymaca.

---

12 Harcourt Fuller and Jada Ben Torres, "Investigating the 'Taíno' Ancestry of the Jamaican Maroons: A New Genetic (DNA), Historical, and Multidisciplinary Analysis and Case Study of the Accompong Town Maroons," *Canadian Journal of Latin American and Caribbean Studies* 43 (2018): 47-78.

The Streets of St. John's
HB

History books have told us that ports were filled with white English and Irish people whose skin would have been especially pale in the grey, foggy, and cool climate.

"I think Newfoundland's ports looked very different than we think they did," says Camille Turner. "It was very common for merchant ships to have motley crews. There must have been Black people there." The Slave Voyages Database shows that three times as many African people crossed the Atlantic Ocean as Europeans from the 1500s to the early 1800s.

Over the centuries, Newfoundland's major city, St. John's, was a cosmopolitan mecca.

People and goods of all stripes and stars sailed through the Narrows into St. John's harbour. Goods included people.

Neil Kennedy cites an example from a 1788 shipping record. Twenty ships from Bermuda, carrying about 250 crew members, came to Newfoundland to fish. Bermudian ships were almost exclusively crewed by enslaved Black men. "Those vessels were remarkably successful. They were denied the right to return (to Newfoundland) because of concerns around competition and protecting the fishery. But what's really striking about the evidence is that the locals resented the presence ... and that the slave sailors were especially good at fishing. Most of the commentary reflects that. They learned very quickly and were extremely successful very early on in the fishery. And so pretty clearly ... in part, it's about wage labour. The protection of wage labour against slave labour."

As well, Kennedy adds, there was the salt. Seasonal labourers on shore in Newfoundland used salt for drying and preserving cod. About one-third of that salt came from islands such as Turks and Caicos in the Caribbean, transported north by ships from Bermuda. "So, when you find conch shells sitting on pathways in our ports in Newfoundland, they're likely brought here from the Turks and Caicos Islands by Black Bermudian sailors."

Conch shells. Salt. We needed to talk with someone who knows about the random bits and pieces of Newfoundland and Labrador. That person is Dale Jarvis, a public folklorist with Heritage NL. Jarvis sees a story in everything—from knitting to fishing wharves to paint colours—and when he reads, he is interested in what might be found in the fine print.

"There are numerous accounts in the early newspaper records, for example, of ships coming in with crews of Black sailors," Jarvis says. "I found an interesting reference to a ship that had sort of survived a shipwreck and had come in under a Norwegian captain. And then, almost as a little throwaway line at the end of the article, was this reference that 'all the sailors were Black or were of African origin.'"

Jarvis, too, points out that St. John's was a busy port town, and a place like that always experienced a steady flow of people and goods coming from everywhere. Sailors from all over the world were mixing on wharves and streets and in taverns.

Jarvis has been looking for more clues about the diversity of those 17th- and 18th-century sailors in legal records: "There are often court records of public disturbances on the waterfront. Fights would break out between sailors and sometimes these would be British Navy sailors who were Black, who were then hauled off to the drunk tank and then released back to their ships later."

The waters surrounding Newfoundland and Labrador were very important to the world. Black people, enslaved and otherwise, were a large part of crews that were found in Newfoundland and Labrador waters and ports. There is written evidence of the presence of Black people in early Newfoundland ports.

A Black man's bones, disinterred in Labrador, now rest in a drawer in the basement of The Rooms in St. John's.

"Think about Newfoundland as a node in the Atlantic and think about what it means to remember the people that are a part of this story and are left out," Turner suggests.

The Bermudian Interruption
XMC

Neil Kennedy speaks of the presence of Black Bermudian sailors in Newfoundland as part of the salt trade. There is also evidence that dozens of Bermudian ships of enslaved peoples fished the Grand Banks in 1787 and 1788, in a case that has been called the Bermudian Interruption.

In his 1895 *A History of Newfoundland*, D.W. Prowse shares a colonial record from Jeremiah Coghlan detailing 34 ships of enslaved Bermudians on the Grand Banks. Coghlan considered their presence an "alarming undertaking."[13] The Bermudians raised eyebrows because of who they were, for their exceptional talents—and because their presence on the Grand Banks at the time was illegal.

In 1788, Britain was concerned with excluding anyone from the fishery who did not serve the national interest of increasing the number of capable seamen in the Royal Navy. Particularly, Canadians, Nova Scotians, Bermudians, and Americans were excluded. Two laws led to the Bermudian Interruption: King William's Act of 1699 (Statues 10 and 11), and Palliser's Act of 1776, which regulated the Newfoundland fishery. King William's Act granted freedom to all British subjects to trade, fish, and erect facilities to process their catch and repair boats and gear on shore in Newfoundland. Because the act was issued at the end of the 17th century, when enslaved Africans were considered chattel, enslaved Black Bermudians were technically not British subjects.

---

13   D.W. Prowse, *A History of Newfoundland* (1895; Boulder, 2002), 345.

Enslaved people did not have the right to fish Newfoundland waters, nor land on shore to dry and cure their fish. Why, then, were the enslaved Black Bermudians there? Possibly because they sailed into Newfoundland waters as legal property of British subjects, on boats belonging to their British colonial owners. Bermudians had fished in Newfoundland even before the 1787 and 1788 Bermudian Interruption; while fishing, they are recorded as taking "possession of vacant ship's or admiral's rooms at different parts to the southward of St. John's," hiring "an experienced Master of voyages to manage and inspect the curing of fish, occupying the said fishing rooms in the same manner as British ships are entitled to."[14]

As it concerns the Bermudian Interruption, Palliser's Act introduced a clause that reserved the right to dry fish in and around the bays and harbours of Newfoundland for British subjects, the Irish, and others coming from British Dominions in Europe. It states in the preamble that Great Britain considered the Newfoundland fishery the foremost nursery for acquiring "able and experienced seamen, always ready to man the Royal Navy when occasions arise."[15] The fishery was to be a solely British venture.

For Bermudians, this exclusivity was damning; it made fishing in Newfoundland waters impractical. The distance between the Grand Banks of Newfoundland and Bermuda was too great to carry green fish.[16] It would spoil during the voyage. Even if the green fish did arrive in Bermuda and was still viable, the damp Bermudian climate made curing said fish mostly untenable.

Given the number of Bermudian ships present in Jeremiah Coghlan's report, were Bermudians aware of Palliser's Act? Was

---

14   Prowse, *A History of Newfoundland*, 346
15   Prowse, *A History of Newfoundland*, 344.
16   Prowse, *A History of Newfoundland*, 417.

Palliser's Act crafted in retaliation to other unrecorded Black bodies in the Newfoundland fishery? Or was it purely a shrewd nationalist British business move?

In August 1788, Newfoundland governor John Elliot was shocked to see 19 Bermudian vessels engaged in the Newfoundland fishery as he entered St. John's. The Bermudians had already fished in Grand Banks and dropped off a cargo load of fish in St. John's to be dried and cured. Elliot witnessed the Bermudians bringing their second load of fish cargo to St. John's. He lamented that he did not arrive earlier to refuse them entry, and in his letter to the governor of Bermuda, Elliot stated that he would permit the enslaved Bermudians to stay, land, and dry their fish for the duration of that season, believing the Bermudians were unaware they were contravening Palliser's Act. He urged the governor of Bermuda, however, to warn the sailors against returning to Newfoundland the following year, based on Palliser's Act.

Elliot later defends his actions to Lord Sydney. He states that although the Bermudians were deprived of "most of the privileges enjoyed by vessels arriving from British Dominions in Europe," they were not precluded from "catching fish on the Banks and bringing them into harbours of Newfoundland for sale."[17] Elliot makes us aware of prior practice of allowing enslaved Bermudians in Newfoundland.

Could Elliot's wishes to keep the Bermudians out have been because the Bermudians by 1788 had proven themselves to be serious competition in the fishery and the West Country men of England feared losing their fishing profits?

Thirty-four ships of enslaved Black people on their owners' boats bobbing around Newfoundland were worthy of concern in 1788. The

---

17   Prowse, *A History of Newfoundland*, 417.

Bermudians could outfit their whole operation for much cheaper than the West Country men of England because slavery resulted in a mostly for-profit venture for the ship owners. The enslaved Bermudians learned the ways of the Newfoundland fishery with haste. According to Coughlan, the Bermudians only faltered during bad weather, and the season of 1788 was quite manageable, as they "were greatly favoured by a most uncommon mild moderate season which was a great encouragement to their exertions, and which men, to the surprised of our fishermen, exceeded them in dispatch." They were twice as fast as their English counterparts: "these Blacks rowed their sloops from 2½ to 3 miles per hour and in working in and out of narrow harbours excelled the best of our fishing lugger shallops. No wind prevented them from getting on the Banks. They maneuvered strong winds in the narrows of St. John's better than masters of West Country men banking ships."[18] Ultimately, the Bermudians caught more fish and demanded more share in the markets.

The Bermudian Interruption is an important part of Newfoundland Black history as well as Newfoundland fishing history. Enslaved Bermudians stayed in and around St. John's and the bays and harbours of Newfoundland to process their fish. They slept in beds around Newfoundland. They fished alongside the British and the Irish in Newfoundland waters. They were here.

Were there more enslaved Africans catching fish in Newfoundland waters to feed other enslaved Africans? How much of the fishery relied on the work of exploited, enslaved Africans, like these Bermudians? The Bermudian Interruption opens the Newfoundland fishery to a new line of study.

---

18 Prowse, *A History of Newfoundland*, 346.

Early Newfoundland
HB

Newfoundland may have been rich in cod, and a point of interest in the triangular trade, but compared to other parts of North America, it was an unappealing place to live year-round. The weather was harsh—long winters; short, cool summers; relentless wind. The soil was shallow and not suitable for large-scale farming.

The Indigenous peoples, including the Beothuk in Newfoundland, and the Inuit and Innu in Labrador, who had been living in the area for thousands of years, subsisted on hunting, fishing, and gathering. Many Indigenous peoples had troubling, violent, and fatal interactions with Europeans.

In the 1500s, Portuguese, Spanish, French, and English crews voyaged across the dangerous North Atlantic Ocean to Newfoundland. The crews were made up of a significant number of people of colour, including enslaved Black people. They fished for the lucrative cod, then dried and salted it on Newfoundland and Labrador's rocky shores. Their ships brought the cod back across the Atlantic to European countries, where it was sold and traded for other goods.

After a few decades in the early 1500s, the Portuguese and Spanish focused their colonization efforts on lands farther south. But they continued to fish Newfoundland waters for centuries, and their boats and their crews regularly visited Newfoundland harbours and ports. The English and the French fought over claiming Newfoundland as their own, sending seasonal fishing crews over in the spring, most of whom would return in the fall.

After the last battle of the Seven Years War between England and France in 1763, France ceded North America, including the island of Newfoundland, to the English. The only territories the French retained were the small islands of St. Pierre and Miquelon off the south coast of Newfoundland. Gradually, more Europeans populated Newfoundland year-round.

By 1720, about 3,000 people lived in Newfoundland, and, by 1780, this number had swelled to 10,000.[19] A few women joined the men coming over on ships, and families were started on Newfoundland soil. The Europeans who populated Newfoundland at that time were roughly divided into three groups: English merchants, who controlled the flow of capital; planters, English middlemen who owned boats for fishing and hired crews; and servants, mostly Irish, who crewed fishing vessels and supplied whatever labour was needed, at sea or on land.

The word *plantation*, which is used in descriptions of early Newfoundland settlements, is commonly associated with the transatlantic slave trade. Plantation most often describes large-scale agricultural operations in the southern United States or Caribbean. Tobacco, cotton, and sugar were common crops, which required strenuous human labour to cultivate and harvest. That human labour was supplied mostly by enslaved Black people.

But *plantation* when referring to Newfoundland and Labrador has a different meaning. A Newfoundland plantation describes a small inshore fishing business and settlement of the 1600s and 1700s, settled by fishers and their families who overwintered in Newfoundland. British settlers "planted" themselves in small

---

19   Jerry Bannister, *The Rule of the Admirals: Law, Custom, and Naval Government in Newfoundland, 1699-1832* (University of Toronto Press, 2003), 201.

colonies and communities along the coast. These small fishing-based communities were often called "plantations" or "fishing stations." The English middlemen who owned small boats or ran small fishing crews were called "planters."

England appointed governors, a judicial system was set up with the first fishing admiral to enter port each spring becoming governor, and churches were established. All of this was done by white, northern Europeans. For centuries, hardly any mention or evidence of Black people was present in these Newfoundland and Labrador colonies, fishing stations, and plantations. But wherever there was colonization, there was slavery.

Colonies
HB

Indigenous people have lived year-round in Newfoundland and Labrador for thousands of years. About 400 years ago, they were joined by white, European settlers—the people who survived the dangerous journey across the Atlantic Ocean and braved the harsh Newfoundland conditions to make permanent homes.

For Europeans during the 1500s and early 1600s, Newfoundland and Labrador was primarily a seasonal fishing station. French and Basque fishing crews generally went to the south coast of Labrador and the west and north coasts of Newfoundland. English crews favoured eastern Newfoundland, including the Avalon Peninsula. A few tough workers would overwinter to take care of fishing shacks and other infrastructure in harbours and ports along the coasts.

Both the French and English governments realized that if they wanted to claim the island of Newfoundland and use it as a base to fish for its never-ending supply of cod, they would need their people to live there year-round. Truly colonize it.

The English established a colony in 1610 at Cupers Cove (now Cupids), only two years after the French established the first French colony in Quebec City in 1608, in what is now Canada. Then, in 1621, the British established the Colony of Avalon about 75 kilometres south of St. John's, in what is now known as Ferryland. In 1662, the French set up a colony and military fortifications at Plaisance, now Placentia, on the French shore, about 130 kilometres southwest of St. John's.

Colonization required many workers to construct, maintain, and defend property, to fish, and to farm. Newfoundland was a challenging place to live year-round. People and livestock died of diseases amid the harsh conditions. How would colonizers ever get enough of a grip on this rough piece of rock in the middle of the North Atlantic?

"Certainly they [early colonists] would have been familiar with enslaved people," says Neil Kennedy. "Both free and enslaved sailors of colour would have passed through places like Ferryland and St. John's by the earliest decades."

Afua Cooper and other historians have unearthed documents that trace the sales of enslaved Black people in parts of British and French North America. Some of those known slave owners also lived in early Newfoundland. European colonies worldwide used slave labour to establish their premises and their businesses. Why would European colonies in Newfoundland be any different?

Jamaica: Rebellions and British Rule

XMC

As in Newfoundland, colonizers fought wars to claim ownership and control of Jamaica. The Spanish colonized Jamaica for 161 years, until the British mounted an invasion in 1655. Under the leadership of men such as Oliver Cromwell, Admiral William Penn, and General Robert Venables, British fleets sailed across the clear blue waters of the Caribbean Sea surrounding the jewel in the West Indies.

Amid the British invasion, the Spanish freed their enslaved Africans. Some of these newly freed Africans joined the Spanish in the fight against the British. Some fled to the interiors to form communities, Maroon Towns. These escaped Africans, traditionally deemed the Maroons of Jamaica, were skilled guerrilla warriors. The Maroons were considered the innovators of the slavery resistance that was characteristic of Jamaica during the transatlantic slave trade.

Maroon communities developed a lasting culture, and still exist as a nation within a nation. Maroons may not be easily distinguishable from other Jamaicans by physical appearance, speech patterns, or dress, but Maroons have maintained distinctive cultures. They possess communally owned treaty lands and are politically autonomous. The Maroons have their own religious beliefs, pharmacopoeia which draws from the nature around them, oral traditions, music, dance, languages, and other less tangible cultural practices.

After five years of battles between the two colonial powers, the British wrangled control of the island. Their rule became official with the signing of the Treaty of Madrid in 1670. In 1692, a powerful earthquake destroyed Port Royal, a longstanding port city of piracy in the region.

At the time of Britain's invasion of Jamaica, the transatlantic slave trade had been an established practice, and the Portuguese dominated the race to capture souls for exploitation and profit. As Britain's empire expanded, with the acquisition of Jamaica and other territories in the Americas, so did its need for the free labour of enslaved Africans.

From the moment Cromwell and company captured Jamaica until the abolition of slavery on January 1, 1808, massive ships such as the *Antelope, Roebuck, Sarah, Betsey, Tonyn, Torbay,* and *Friendship*—all Newfoundland-built vessels—brought millions of stolen human beings to shore where a life of damnation awaited.

As Newfoundland had cod, Jamaica had sugar cane.

The English quickly busied themselves with planting and populating Jamaica, in God's name. Tobacco, indigo, and cocoa crops gave way to the behemoth, sugar cane, as the island's primary production, as sugar was easily sold in England. By 1739, Jamaica had 430 estates, up from 57 in 1673. The enslaved Africans were the only labour force cheap enough to keep the booming sugar industry profitable for the colonists. They had no choice in the means or methods of production, in the products produced or their unenviable position in the economic system. No choice in the food given to them so they could then turn around and be forced to provide for the world.

The world grew more addicted to sugar, and Jamaica had the perfect conditions for growing sugar cane, a crop introduced by the Spanish. Men from England erected great houses on large hills overlooking acres and acres of their white gold. These elaborate houses stood as a celebration of the plantation owners' power and wealth from which they watched their fellow man toil relentlessly over oversized blades of grass.

Farther down, the enslaved Africans lived in huts in the communities they were forced to create. Fed by codfish from Newfoundland, the enslaved Africans were forced into unrelenting and unending backbreaking labour, day in and day out. Families rarely stayed intact. When their bodies could no longer work, or were burned alive from weeding the sugar cane, or they fell into a vat of boiling sugar, or had a limb amputated by the vicious production cycle, or were murdered during a daring attempt at freedom, another boat—possibly made by residents of Newfoundland—filled with more stolen souls, replaced those that were lost. All in the name of sugar and money. Everyone but the enslaved benefitted from the millions of African people traded throughout the period of the transatlantic slave trade.

The National Museum of African American History and Culture reports that the life expectancy of the imported enslaved African working in colonial sugar plantations, such as those in Jamaica, was seven years. Many died within their first year from being overworked or from their living conditions.

The Maroons laid the blueprint for rebellions on the island; they can be considered the original freedom fighters. Twenty-one slave rebellions were recorded in Jamaica over 325 years from the beginning of slavery on the island to full emancipation, more than in all other British colonized islands combined. The First Maroon War lasted from 1730 to 1740. The great military commander and chief Queen Nanny of the Maroons, the only female national hero, led many thousands of enslaved Africans in a valiant battle against the British.

Armed with exceptional knowledge of the island's mountainous interior terrain and brilliant guerrilla warfare tactics, the Maroons forced the British to grant the Leeward Maroons affiliated with

Kojo, in the west central interior of Jamaica, political autonomy in 1739, and the Windward Maroons of eastern Jamaica led by Queen Nanny, and Quao, in the Blue Mountains, theirs in 1740. The Maroons pledged to stop fighting the British and to help settle the problem of runaway slaves. This agreement formed a rift within the Maroon community; some Maroons did not agree with participating in the exploitation of others.

Tacky's unsuccessful rebellion in 1760 rocked the island's planter class. Tacky, an African chief, led supporters to take over plantations, killing the white plantation owners in the process. In 1791, information spread orally throughout Jamaica of the large-scale enslaved rebellion taking place in Saint Domingue, now Haiti. The news of the Haitian Revolution found attentive listeners and caused hundreds of enslaved Africans in Jamaica to participate in island-wide unrest from 1791 until 1792.

In 1795, relations between the Trelawny Town Maroons and the British representative government soured and erupted in the Second Maroon War. Despite their courageous battle under the leadership of such men as James Palmer, the Maroons were unable to secure victory.

The Second Maroon War ended in 1796, and 600 Maroon men, women, and children were shipped from Jamaica to Nova Scotia, where they faced racism, attempts at forced assimilation into Christianity, ill treatment, and harsh winters. While in Nova Scotia, the Maroons joined Nova Scotia militia units. The Maroons helped construct Government House and the third Halifax Citadel.

But, dissatisfied with their treatment, and desiring to be anywhere warmer, the Maroons petitioned the House of Commons of Great Britain on January 4, 1799, stating, "the soil of Nova Scotia will never answer to transplant Maroons in, nor will they ever thrive where the Pine Apple does not."[20] The Trelawny Town Leeward Maroons departed Halifax for Sierra Leone, West Africa, in 1800, as they were denied re-entry to Jamaica. They were still considered to be a destabilizing force to British colonialism.

In 1807, the Slave Trade Act passed by the British parliament abolished the slave trade. After March 1, 1808, the transportation of slaves across the Atlantic to Jamaica was forbidden. The act did not end the practice of slavery; that would not happen for decades. By this point, some 2 million people had been traded to Jamaica, not including the many thousands who had died on slave ships as they journeyed to the Caribbean from West Africa. According to the Slave Voyages Database, 1,885 enslaved Africans were delivered to Jamaica by Newfoundland-built ships.

The Christmas rebellion of 1831/1832, which began on Kensington Estate in St. James parish, was led by Sam Sharpe, who has been named a national hero of Jamaica. Also known as the Baptist War, this revolt urged the British parliament to vote in 1833 to "abolish" colonial slavery.

---

20 Jeffrey A. Fortin, "'Blackened Beyond Our Native Hue': Removal, Identity and the Trelawney Maroons on the Margins of the Atlantic World, 1796-1800," *Citizenship Studies* 10, no. 1 (2006): 5–34, quotation at 5.

Calvert's Ferryland
HB

We needed to find out more about what it took to set up a successful colony by European standards in early Newfoundland. We met with archaeologist Dr. Barry Gaulton at the Colony of Avalon. The Colony of Avalon, considered the best preserved early English colonial site in North America, is in Ferryland, a fishing town of about 400 people, an hour's drive along the coast from St. John's.

The people who live in the small towns on this road, also known as the Irish Loop, speak with accents and turns of phrase that are nearly identical to that heard in rural southeast Ireland. People around here even *look* Irish—pale skin, blue eyes, and red hair. Locals are proud of their Irish roots and cultural connections.

More than the Irish lived on this shore. There were people who were darker of complexion and who had a much darker history.

Ferryland looks like the setting of a fairy tale. Fingers of early morning fog parted to reveal a snug harbour, with a rocky beach at its shoreline, surrounded by low green hills. You can order a picnic lunch and enjoy it on the grassy point by the red lighthouse. In the spring, magnificent icebergs sometimes float by.

Gaulton is down by The Pool, a sheltered area of the inner harbour. "Jim Tuck, the [Colony of Avalon's] founding archaeologist and my mentor, used to say that everyone but the Vikings came here," says Gaulton. Tuck was also head of the team that investigated and excavated the remains of W.H.

There is evidence that the Beothuk, Newfoundland's early and extinct Indigenous people, spent time in Ferryland. Early European explorers and their crews, from at least several countries, passed through this port.

The most stunning remains of a community, though, are from the Colony of Avalon archaeological site—4 acres of excavated 17th-century stone walls, a cobblestoned street, building foundations, and recreated historic fences and gardens. "Every element of a well-set-up English colony existed here," Gaulton says.

Gaulton started working here 30 years ago as an archaeology student, and, in addition to his position at Memorial University, he is now the Colony of Avalon's chief archaeologist. He loves this place and that the people of Ferryland have worked side by side with archaeologists to explore, preserve, and tell the world about the Colony of Avalon. So far, the townspeople and archaeologists have uncovered about a third of the 17th-century settlement. There is much more to uncover about who lived and passed through here.

The Colony of Avalon was founded in 1621 by Englishman Sir George Calvert, also known as Lord Baltimore. Calvert was determined to establish a permanent English colony in the New World. This spot seemed ideal. It was conveniently located near the codfishing grounds, it had a rocky beach suitable for salting and drying cod, and it had green fields that looked like they could be developed into productive farmland. Workers spent seven years building this community. By the time Calvert and his entourage arrived in 1628, the colony was thriving.

Gaulton walks us through the excavations on the 4-acre site. This was no primitive outpost but a sophisticated English colonial town. The Colony had all the modern conveniences of 1621—a large, two-storey stone mansion for Calvert and his family, stables, a customs house on the waterfront, even the 1621 version of plumbing: a privy that was flushed by the sea. There was a brewhouse and a bakery, and smaller quarters for servants and other lower-class residents. In total, in the 1620s, about 100 people lived there.

For its day, life in the Colony of Avalon was surprisingly open-minded: Calvert allowed the lower-class Irish workers to openly practice their Catholic faith and have their own worship services. But, given that wherever there was colonization, there was slavery—were Black enslaved people here, too?

Neil Kennedy thinks it is likely: "It would be very surprising to me if enslaved people weren't present in places like Ferryland or Cupids in the 17th century. [Enslaved Black people] were ubiquitous in the English colonial world for a few reasons, one being that the English wanted to emulate the Spanish, and one element of Spanish success in the Americas was associated with slavery."

At the Colony of Avalon, Gaulton and his crew have determined that ships from Europe, America, and the Caribbean were regular visitors to the port. For Kennedy, that is another indicator that Black people were there: "We also know that people of colour were quite common on the merchant vessels of the 17th century, more so in the 18th century; these were multi-ethnic crews. Even if we are not necessarily able to identify enslaved people in Ferryland, people in Ferryland would have been familiar with enslaved people. Both free and enslaved sailors of colour would have passed through Ferryland and St. John's by the early decades [of the 17th century]."

The workers at the Colony of Avalon have discovered much about how the English and Irish settlers lived there. But it is becoming clearer, as Camille Turner notes, the thriving early ports of Newfoundland were probably quite multicultural.

People from all over the world wandered around on the wharves of the Colony, and at least some of them had to be enslaved Black people. As Turner, Kennedy, Cooper, and others have shown, it would have been unusual for those ships *not* to carry enslaved Black people.

We linger in the large, excavated foundation of Baltimore's Mansion, the main stone house. It would have been a spacious, two-storey building, with windows overlooking the harbour, a big kitchen hearth, a comfortable home befitting the status of the Calvert family. We lean against the walls of the Butter Room, a storage area for supplies that came in large barrels called butts. This was executive housing, 1620s style. It was the kind of house designed for people who would have had servants. Would the Calverts, people of high status, have owned domestic slaves?

The research conducted at the Colony of Avalon has not revealed much about the Calvert family's entourage. All of us, including Gaulton, have realized that history is as much about what has *not* been written down, or recorded, as it is about what is found in ledgers, excavated from the earth, or written about in history books.

Alas, Lord Baltimore's stay at the Colony of Avalon was short.

When the Calverts arrived in the middle of a gentle 1621 summer, locals assured them that the weather year-round at the Colony of Avalon was quite reasonable. That is a lie that Newfoundlanders have continued to tell newcomers for centuries.

After coping with one brutal winter, the Calverts had had enough. Rumour has it that Lady Baltimore insisted that they leave. Whatever the reason, the Calverts fled south, to the gentler climate of the eastern seaboard of the United States and founded what would become the city of Baltimore. But that was not the end of the Colony of Avalon.

David Kirke saw an opportunity—a colony ready for him to take over.

Kirke's Ferryland
HB

Shortly after the Calverts departed the Colony of Avalon on a voyage between Canada and England, David Kirke stopped by Ferryland. An English military man and merchant who assisted in the surrender of the French in Quebec in 1629, Kirke was also a known slave trader.

"In Quebec, he sold his nine-year-old male slave to a French clerk," says Barry Gaulton. "In light of that reference, it wouldn't surprise me if David Kirke also brought enslaved Africans with him in 1638 when he arrived in Newfoundland to live specifically at the Colony of Avalon."

Documentation of enslaved Black people in the earliest Newfoundland colonies is elusive. Even when documents exist, Gaulton says, it is difficult to prove if Kirke took enslaved Black people to the Colony of Avalon. "However, if you wanted to make that connection between previous slave ownership and later slave ownership, then that example of David Kirke certainly would be one of the earliest." There is no reason, according to Gaulton, that Kirke would have done anything differently in Newfoundland than he would have in Quebec.

In Ferryland, Kirke saw a nearly move-in-ready colony—a community with thriving fishing operations, significant infrastructure, and even a grand house for him and his family. In 1637, King Charles I of England passed the commercial rights to the colony to Kirke, with several of Kirke's brothers on board as partners.

Kirke, now Sir David Kirke, his wife, Lady Sara Kirke, and his family moved into Baltimore's Mansion, and renamed the colony

Pool Plantation. Kirke became the governor of Ferryland and of all of Newfoundland. "They [the Kirkes] would have had all the trappings of wealthy merchants with status," Gaulton says.

Kirke was a ruthless businessman who turned the colony at Ferryland into a successful, even thriving, business and community. He taxed foreign vessels docking in port; he taxed local fishers for their wharfside infrastructure, or fishing rooms; and he taxed local business owners and residents. He acquired monopolies on goods entering and leaving many parts of Newfoundland.

Kirke and his family had material wealth. Gaulton and his team have dug up evidence of a high-end 17th-century life: monogrammed dinnerware, gold jewellery, wax seals for letters and important papers, and children's toys.

Kirke wielded economic and political power, even having his own currency made. Gaulton and his team have excavated many coins of different sizes, presumably indicating different values—with the initials D.K. engraved on them. Kirke enjoyed about 15 lucrative years in Newfoundland, but eventually, his business practices and British politics caught up with him. He was summoned to England in 1651, charged with tax offences, and imprisoned, where he died in 1654.

Meanwhile, the Kirkes continued to run Pool Plantation in Ferryland. Lady Sara Kirke, Sir David's wife, and her sister, Lady Frances Hopkins, turned Pool Plantation into the largest fishing operation on the English part of Newfoundland's shores.

"We know Sara Kirke and Frances Hopkins brought to Ferryland slave-produced products like sugar, tobacco, oranges, and lemons," Neil Kennedy says. "So, we have these bits of evidence of the involvement very early on of settlers in Newfoundland with the products of slavery, and the related commodity trades that were associated with slavery." Under the control of these two women, a tide of people, money, and goods from all over the world flowed in and out of the harbour.

Gaulton and his team have excavated tobacco pipes from the United States and Jamaica—nations which used enslaved labour heavily in the tobacco industry—ceramic plates and bowls from slave-trading Portugal, toys and walking canes from slave-trading England, and gold jewellery from Africa, where slaves were abducted.

Under the two women, the colony thrived. It supported at least 100 residents: English fishers and their families, Irish servants and other low-status workers, as well as many sailors who came ashore from the ships arriving in the busy harbour. By the time Lady Kirke retired in 1679, the colony was established and secure.

Could any of this have been done without the use of enslaved Black labour?

It was highly unusual for a colony like this to be run by women. And from what we know about such communities of its time, it would be highly unusual for it to function without unpaid, enslaved labour.

"It [slavery] was the cost of doing business in a colonial setting and specifically in the New World," Gaulton says. The challenge is finding the evidence.

Record-keeping of any kind in 17th-century Newfoundland was spotty at the best of times. Few documents of any sort connected to Newfoundland settlements during Calvert's and Kirke's time exist. However, a handful of references to Black enslaved people is found in documents from the English settlement in St. John's and the French settlement in Placentia at that time.

From the little they know of enslaved Black people's lives, Gaulton thinks they would do work similar to what white servants did: "Household talks, cooking, cleaning, tending the garden, tending livestock, caring for children."

That was likely the work. But as for their lives, we know less than that. Because Black people were regarded as property, not people, it is even harder to find evidence of them.

Gaulton is staking his hopes on finding more evidence of Black residents of Ferryland during the Kirke's time in something that everyone, regardless of status, created. "I love garbage! If someone looked through your garbage for a year, they would probably find out a lot about you."

Much of the garbage that has already been excavated at the Colony of Avalon is now stored at the Colony's visitor centre, a converted school building a few hundred metres from the Colony. It has a museum on the first floor and a working archaeology lab on the second floor. About half a million objects have been found and labelled, from tiny bits of glass to slate roofing tiles to large building stones. Many of these objects are carefully stored in cardboard filing boxes in special rooms.

Staff are constantly piecing together these objects and their history. On our visit, one worker was patiently gluing together small bits of pottery to form a monogrammed ceramic plate: a colourful piece of custom-made Portuguese dinnerware. The plate looked like it was waiting to be filled with roasted meat, gravy, and vegetables. But pieces of that plate are missing. It cannot hold a meal.

Like those plates with the missing pieces, we do not have the complete story of every person of every status that lived at the Colony of Avalon. That leaves Gaulton hungry for answers: "How do we find these silent voices? How do we get at them?"

Gaulton and other researchers have started to look for the silent voices of 17th-century British colonies in unlikely places. Places such as the last will and testament of John Benger.

Benger's Ferryland
HB

Barry Gaulton discovered the 1791 will of John Benger at the National Archives of the United Kingdom:[21] "It is here that we find the first solid evidence of an enslaved Black person living in Ferryland." Benger was a prominent English settler in Ferryland, a planter who ran a large fishing establishment in the community.

Benger's will, written in an English script and 18th-century English legal jargon, is difficult for modern eyes to decipher. Gaulton has slowly and patiently picked through it: "It states that he had a number of enslaved individuals as part of his household as far back as 1791. He mentions his slave, Sarah; Sarah's husband, Sancho; and their children, Jack, Nancy, and Stephen, and his wish that they be freed upon his death." Benger's will appears to provide some money to sustain the family of people he owned. "He says he provides £5 per annum for their sustenance to maintain them. He also tries to suggest that perhaps they can find employment in other households in Ferryland."

What happened to Sarah, Sancho, Jack, Nancy, and Stephen?

Gaulton's team discovered that at least Stephen, as a freed man, moved to another settlement in Newfoundland: "Stephen went a couple of communities south of Ferryland to Fermeuse, where he made a living as a fisherman for a few years. We don't know what happened to him after that." As for the rest of Stephen's family,

---

21 Will of John Benger of Ferryland, Newfoundland, North America, translated by Barry Gaulton. Records of the Prerogative Court of Canterbury, PROB 11/1227/235, The National Archives (UK).

Gaulton and his team have, as of yet, found no clues as to what happened to them after the death of John Benger. Did they stay in Ferryland? Were they freed? What does being freed mean, if you are an enslaved Black person in Newfoundland in 1791?

We left Ferryland and drove 14 kilometres south to Fermeuse, a smaller fishing community than Ferryland. Its harbour is quiet but its wharf is packed with moored fishing boats. It is still a thriving fishing community. In the 1790s, Fermeuse was a short sail from Ferryland, just a few harbours south.

There are no museums in Fermeuse. There is no trace of a Black man named Stephen who lived and worked there for a few years in the 1790s.

In Ferryland, Gaulton and Neil Jordan, another long-time archaeologist at the Colony of Avalon site, spend their downtime rebuilding the excavated walls. Walls that were built in the 1600s and buried for centuries are now exposed to the harsh Newfoundland weather again. They get heaved out of place by the freezing and thawing that happens during Newfoundland winters.

As Gaulton and Jordan rebuild walls, they are also rebuilding our ideas of what the Colony of Avalon was like and who lived here.

In the popular retelling of Newfoundland and Labrador's history and culture, especially along Newfoundland's southern shore, the story of the early years is about the English and the Irish, those who came with their families and built a living based on the cod fishery.

"You don't hear about the everyday fisherman," says Gaulton. "You don't hear about servants. You don't hear about enslaved individuals. I've been here 30 years, focusing on the English and Irish. It's time that we right that wrong and include everyone else."

No Fairy Tales in Ferryland
XMC

Before George Calvert made investments towards colonial development in Ferryland and Ireland, he invested in the Virginia Company, a British trading company which was created in 1606 to colonize the eastern region of America. Calvert was also an investor in the East India Company,[22] created in 1600 as a monopolistic trading body to exploit East and Southeast Asia and India. As an agent of British imperialism, the company wanted a share in the East Indian spice trade. In the early 1620s, the company turned to the labour of enslaved people and traded people from Indonesia and West Africa but concentrated on those from East Africa, Mozambique, and Madagascar.

Calvert believed in colonialism. He played an active part in the creation of colonies in the New World and in the mechanisms used to perpetuate the systems of exploitation that made spreading imperialism possible.

In 1627, Calvert sailed across the Atlantic to inspect his investment in colonialism in Ferryland, Newfoundland. He found a community that had taken years and countless hours of expert labour to build; he returned in 1628, but left the colony forever the following year. Calvert was invested in prolific slave-trading companies, but there is no mention of his enlisting the labour of enslaved people in

---

22   Aaron F. Miller, "Avalon and Maryland: A Comparative Historical Archaeology of the Seventeenth Century New World Provinces of the Lords Baltimore (1621-1644)" (PhD diss., Memorial University of Newfoundland, 2013), 1, 42-43.

the construction of his colony of Avalon or his voyages across the Atlantic. However, the slave trade had been active for over a century when Calvert sailed into Newfoundland with his family, ready to call the island home.

The Colony of Avalon excavation site in Ferryland reveals the wonders that settlers constructed for Calvert: roads, canals, elaborate seaport constructions, specialty buildings. It was a fully serviced town, a distinct hierarchy with the Calverts as the head, skilled labourers, and the lower class. We do not know if the lower class was composed of any Black people.

David Kirke and his wife, Sara Kirke, had turned Ferryland into a thriving port town. A spot of continuous international trade. History books show no record of a trade of people. But colonialization went hand in hand with the exploited labour of Black people. Was Newfoundland the exception to the rule? If there were slaves, were they transient? Were they sold at a harbour and taken elsewhere?

A 1626 port record refers to the sale of an enslaved person in St. John's that year. It does not indicate if that person went on to live their life in Newfoundland. Additionally, Thomas Oxford of St. John's, Newfoundland, a man of high social standing, possessed a "negro house-servant—a most aristocratic appendage" in the latter half of the 17th century. In a footnote of history, we learn that this enslaved Black person was "valued worth 60 pounds sterling"[23] by the Newfoundland Board of Trade. Oxford's house servant was forcibly taken from him by West Country men. This Black person was property, an appendage, his life and stories boiled down to a footnote of history.

Were the Black people recorded in Newfoundland history the only ones on the island at the time? Or was it commonplace to

---

23   Prowse, *A History of Newfoundland*, 176.

disregard their presence as they were not considered people—much like the Beothuk on the Avalon?

Barry Gaulton and archaeologists have found proof of the Beothuk, the annihilated Indigenous people of Newfoundland, in Ferryland, while history previously led us to believe that they did not frequent the area. In 1986, small quantities of Beothuk materials were found stratigraphically beneath one of Ferryland's dry-laid stone walls.[24] A Beothuk hearth has been uncovered, and Beothuk bifaces and projectile points have been recovered from the archaeological site. Further excavation of the Beothuk hearth in 2015 produced over 100 grape seeds and several beach peas. As grapes do not grow wild in Newfoundland, the Beothuk could have only acquired them in the form of raisins or poorly strained wine, suggesting friendly contact with European newcomers.[25] These findings suggest that Beothuk contact with European newcomers was more common and longer than previously thought.

I have heard many statements about Newfoundland and slavery that have shocked me. One such statement is that the poor Irish settlers, like those found in Ferryland, and other outport communities, like those along the Irish Loop, were the slaves of the British and the merchants on Water Street. But there is a logical error in this line of thought: the poor settlers in Newfoundland were not enslaved; the two groups of people are not comparable. There was a distinguishable difference in the lived realities of the poor settlers in Newfoundland and the enslaved Africans in Jamaica and Newfoundland within the colonial system of the time.

---

24   Rick Gaulton, "Early Historic Beothuk Indian Evidence from Ferryland, Newfoundland (CgAf-2)" (BA Honour's essay, Memorial University of Newfoundland, 2001), 4.
25   Barry C. Gaulton and Catherine Hawkins, "Interim Report: Ferryland (CgAf-2). Permit # 15.20," 2015.

Gaulton's unearthing of John Benger's will proves that enslaved people led full lives in Newfoundland. Upon his death, Benger freed his "negroes" in Ferryland. Benger's "negroes" were a family of five people. Sarah and Sancho, and "Sarah's children honor who I desire may be sent to Mr. Robert Carter Ferryland. The Boy Jack, the Girl Nancy and the Boy Stephen all free and to be maintained in a manner as poor children are to be sent to some Trade or as Servants so as to get their Bread or if agreeable to the family of the late Wm Dobell to take them into the Kitchen."[26] Benger bequeaths his family of enslaved people as one would a favourite jacket or pair of earrings to a sibling. Parents are separated from their children upon his death, a common slave trade occurrence and a sign of the disrespect for Black families.

While the working-class poor in Newfoundland had the ability to start families that were not systematically dismembered. Enslaved peoples "lived with the perpetual possibility of separation through the sale of one or more family members."[27]

Even from beyond the grave, Benger controls these humans: Sancho is guaranteed an annual stipend for life, unless he were to fall into the service of another family. Sarah receives a stipend only if she abstains from marriage or having another child. Benger leaves no stipend for the children. They are left to the mercy of their new bosses. Were any of them truly free after Benger's death?

Records reveal that Stephen eventually moved to Fermeuse and became a fisher. We do not know what happened to Jack, Nancy, Sarah, or Sancho. History has forgotten them, their story restricted to a paragraph in a document that is unreadable by most today.

---

26 Will of John Benger of Ferryland.
27 Heather Andrea Williams, "How Slavery Affected African American Families," Freedom's Story, TeacherServe©, National Humanities Center, https://nationalhumanitiescenter.org/tserve/freedom/1609-1865/essays/aafamilies.htm.

When I hear all this from Barry Gaulton, I become morose, quiet. I cannot celebrate the historical Black presence in Newfoundland—because it is a history of slavery. Those who wrote down the history and those who taught it orally chose not to include Sarah, Sancho, Jack, Nancy, and Stephen. Benger and his incrimination of other community members in the practice of slavery suggests that Newfoundland was not an exception to the rule of colonialism and its reliance of the labour of enslaved people.

Gaulton says that the records were poorly kept in the early days of Ferryland and that lack of proof on paper is helpful to the forgetting. No story, no case.

I have so many questions about Sancho, Sarah, Jack, Nancy, and Stephen. How many trips across the Atlantic did they all have to endure? Were they the only enslaved peoples in Ferryland? Did Benger have Sancho, Jack, and Stephen perform manual labour in his fish plantation, while, in patriarchal fashion, Sarah and Nancy focused on the familial work of enslaved domestics?

Black women are nowhere to be found in Newfoundland history books. How many generations of Newfoundland babies were cared for and nurtured by forgotten loving Black hands? Black women who endured much agony but still held their oppressors gently. It is good to know that Stephen had a career and moved to Fermeuse, away from where he had been kept as an enslaved boy. But what did that freedom look like?

I look around Ferryland and Fermeuse, and there is a heavy feeling in both places now. The air is not any saltier and neither am I. While I cannot revel in this new information, I can think of Sarah, Sancho, Jack, Nancy, and Stephen when I think of Ferryland and all the people who helped make Newfoundland what it is.

In July 2022, Heather and I visited other early sites of

colonialism on the Avalon Peninsula. In Placentia, formerly the colonial settlement of Plaisance, the only sign of Blackness, past or present, was a caricature statue of a little Black boy placed proudly in the middle of a lawn. Unfortunately, it was not my first time seeing one of those racist lawn ornaments in outport Newfoundland.

If Newfoundlanders knew more about their entire history, would they be more sensitive and attuned to the insidiousness of racism? Would they display Black lawn ornaments?

Domestic Property
HB

By the 1700s, English settlement had taken hold on the island of Newfoundland. The cod fishery on the Grand Banks was booming, and cod as a commodity remained in high demand. St. John's and communities on the Southern Shore were growing. By the 1730s, several thousand non-Indigenous people lived on the island of Newfoundland, most of whom were English and Irish.

"It seems quite clear to me, and I'm sure to most, that the practice of slavery not only was acceptable, but in some cases, it was quite commonplace, in various European settlements in the province," says Barry Gaulton. "I guess if you were to look back 300 to 400 years ago, I think it [slavery] was, in many cases, generally accepted." An early example is from the French colony of Plaisance: "There's a 1677 reference to a Black female slave [there] owned by a European settler."

Mentions of Black people as property surface in the wills of other early English settlers in Newfoundland. Dale Jarvis cites the will of John Ryan, an American who settled in Newfoundland and started Newfoundland's first newspaper, the *Royal Gazette*. Ryan died in 1847, and when his will was read, his wish to free his slave was indicated. "He [Ryan] talks about bequeathing his female slave, Dinah, her freedom immediately upon his death. We also know from his will that Dinah had two children, Cornelius and Rachel. And in Ryan's will it was established that they [the children] should be retained in his family or bound out to some credible person until they came to the age of 21. And we don't really know what happened to any of them."

Jarvis has also scoured the fine print of other historical records: "When we look at the colonial records from the 1800s, which were often broken down by race when we are talking about population, the columns for coloured people or Black people are often just blank, completely blank, no entries of any kind. Often, census takers would just not record them as people in the records."

Jarvis and Neil Kennedy have found clues in baptismal and burial records from the Church of England parish in St. John's that identify nine people of colour who lived in St. John's during the 17th century. Those records contain no information about their identities or their work. One parish record from 1816 noted the burial of a Negro woman, also named Dinah.

Legal records also occasionally yield clues. One 1777 document housed in The Rooms Provincial Archives states that "Governor Montagu revoked the liquor licence of John Phillips, a publican, for beating a black servant-girl."[28]

Kennedy has filled in some of the gaps with information about this young woman through a colonial secretary's book of that time. Her name: Katherine. She belonged to John Phillips, whom the book identified as a commercial agent, likely an American. "She tries to flee his house, and the governor tries to intervene as a justice of the peace to protect Katherine by placing her in jail. But Phillips won't allow her to leave his house. She's eventually rescued by the justice of the peace and given her freedom again." This, Kennedy points out, confirmed that she was an enslaved woman. No other information was given.

---

28 Bannister, *The Rule of the Admirals*, 201.

How many Black people, enslaved and otherwise, lived in Newfoundland and Labrador? "When there are several, there's very likely a lot more. I think that recognition would be an important step," Gaulton says.

"We have a duty to people like Katherine to recover these stories," Kennedy adds. "To try and recreate the kinds of lived experiences that she faced, and to not reduce her to simply a name in a ledger, but to try and more fully imagine her experience and her life."

Katherine. Dinah. Sancho. Sarah. Jack. Nancy. Stephen. Dinah. Cornelius. Rachel.

Dinah, Cornelius, and Rachel
HB

Emily Davidson is trying to find out more about the mother, son, and daughter of a Black family living in early 19th-century St. John's. Davidson, a research assistant at the Institute for the Study of Canadian Slavery at the Nova Scotia College of Art and Design (NSCAD), in Halifax, Nova Scotia, first encountered Dinah, Cornelius, and Rachel while researching newspaper publishers of that era in what are now known as Canada's Atlantic provinces. She realized that this small family could help develop a better picture of Black people in what is now eastern Canada after coming across Dinah's name through her research on John Ryan, the American-born publisher of the *Royal Gazette*.

Ryan's will, written while he was living in St. John's in 1814, instructs his executors to manumit, or release from slavery, Dinah, upon his death. Additionally, Dinah's children, Cornelius and Rachel, should continue to be enslaved by Ryan's family until they reached the age of 21, when they too could be manumitted.

To piece together their story, Davidson backtracked to New Brunswick, in 1806.

Before Ryan moved to Newfoundland, he had bought a Black woman named Dinah from James Taylor, also a printer and publisher, in New Brunswick. There is no indication of Dinah's place of origin or how many times she had been sold. After Ryan took ownership of Dinah, he placed an advertisement in the *Royal Gazette* of Saint John, New Brunswick, on December 24, 1806, as a pre-emptive warning about Dinah's possible escape or theft. It listed

Dinah's physical description, with a warning to "all persons against attempting in future to seduce from his Service his Female Negro Slave DINAH. (for whom he has a good legal title)."[29]

"What is going on, that before she runs away, he's warning his white buddies not to take her away from him?" Davidson wonders. "That level of control is really intense."

As for Dinah's life in St. John's, Davidson's research shows that Dinah, with her children Cornelius and Rachel, would have been the enslaved family serving the Ryan family and business. They would have lived in the Ryan family home, doing whatever needed to be done—cooking and cleaning, child rearing, subsistence farming, labouring at the printing business.

Life in Newfoundland at that time was harsh for everyone, and for a Black woman, it would have been especially foreign and isolating.

But compared to the lives of enslaved Black people who endured the horrors of the Middle Passage across the Atlantic from Africa, or who toiled on cotton and sugar plantations in the United States or the Caribbean, could Dinah, Cornelius, and Rachel have had relatively decent lives?

As Davidson says, enslaved domestic workers living in what is now Atlantic Canada, under the same roof as their owners, did not live a safe and cozy life: "What other sorts of violence does that open people up to? This is not a benign form of human interaction." Dinah and her children would have very little space or privacy, which would make them vulnerable to violence, including sexual violence, from others living closely with them.

As for Dinah's children, Cornelius and Rachel, who was their

---

29 John Ryan, "CAUTION," *Royal Gazette* (Saint John, New Brunswick), December 24, 1806; cited in *Black Slavery in the Maritimes: A History in Documents,* by Harvey Amani Whitfield (Broadview Press, 2018), 68.

father? Could it have been John Ryan? One—or more—of Ryan's sons? An enslaved or free Black man in the community? An Indigenous person? A white person of low status? So far, no one has found any answers to these questions. Such information about enslaved Black people was not documented in Newfoundland at that time.

"What is she [Dinah] going to do as a free Black person in St. John's in 1814? Without her children? Is she going to have to stay with the Ryan family in order to stay with her children? It's a plan which is still quite brutal." As Davidson dug into the history of Dinah, her family, and John Ryan, each piece of information revealed more questions than answers.

Ryan's will was dated 1814, yet historical records show that he died in 1847. What happened to Dinah, Cornelius, and Rachel between those years?

In 1834, Britain's parliament abolished slavery across the British empire, and that included Newfoundland. If Dinah, Cornelius, and Rachel were alive, as freed people in 1834, they still would have had very low status in their community. Where could they go? Would they have had to stay with the Ryan family anyway?

Dale Jarvis had mentioned a record of a Black woman named Dinah buried in the Church of England cemetery in St. John's in 1816. Was that the same Dinah?

"What we don't know is what actually happened," says Davidson. Dinah was a common name for Black women at that time, so it might be the same Dinah, or it could be another Black woman named Dinah living in St. John's. "I remain unconvinced that there were as few Black people as the narrative suggested. I wonder if there weren't more."

Even if Dinah, Cornelius, or Rachel lived long enough to be freed, it would be next to impossible to find out anything about them. As Davidson notes, most of the recorded accounts of Black people in Atlantic Canada refer to them as property: enslaved people. Freed Black people would have been of low community status, likely not paying taxes or owning any property; therefore, written mentions of them, other than in court documents, would have been rare.

Ryan was not the only newspaper publisher to hold enslaved Black people. This, Davidson discovered, was a common practice among early Canadian newspaper owners. Publishing ads warning white readers about escaped slaves was as much a part of early newspapers as advertisements about soap.

"This has been a real shift in my thinking of the history of print, as a weapon of domination," Davidson says. "As a white person in this field of research, [I'm trying to understand] how did white people think this was normal?"

Enslaved Domestics
XMC

"*If* there *was* slavery in Newfoundland, it might not have been *that bad.*" I have heard this sentiment voiced in Newfoundland during the scant number of times the topic of slavery in the province arises in conversation. Two things are at play here. One, the supposition that there was no slavery in Newfoundland. That Newfoundland was the only British colony during the slave trade that did not use the labour of enslaved Africans. And second, that if there was slavery here, that it was, somehow, not *that bad.*

I believe that when there was slavery, it was horrendous, repulsive, and inhumane. The overarching notion of the nice Newfoundlander has made the supposition of slavery in Newfoundland being *not bad* as popular as the now debunked belief that slavery did not happen on the island.

Any romanticization of domestic slavery is absurd. In Jamaica, there were field slaves and also house slaves—the domestics, women, often lighter skinned than those enslaved in the fields. House slaves, with their legacy of *desirable* house colour complexion, were the property of their masters and his household as much as their brothers, sisters, and kin outside in the fields were property too. Away from the blazing sun, in the privacy of the home their abuse and dehumanization were locked away behind closed doors; they were isolated, doomed by the severe power imbalance and forced into intimacy with their masters. Africans made to do domestic work were still enslaved and subject to a violent racist regime.

There was domestic slavery in Newfoundland. *Royal Gazette* founder John Ryan's 1814 will shows that much. It is noteworthy that this will was never executed, as he died in 1847 after the abolition of slavery.

According to Dr. Charmaine Nelson, art historian and Director of Slavery North Initiative at the University of Massachusetts, Amherst, Ryan's will represents the mindset of the slave-owning class in Newfoundland at the time. This class, Nelson says, was not relegated to the rich; the acquisition of enslaved people was not restricted to the merchant class. The slave trade pierced all tiers of society in small port towns. The print shop, like the one that published Ryan's *Royal Gazette*, was used to tell other whites about fugitive enslaved people, as well as their constant advertisements of the sale of enslaved people. Printers, butchers, and locksmiths enslaved individuals as apprentices in their shops.

Ryan's will disregards Dinah's family. Posthumously, Ryan planned to control the life of this woman and her children. He was ready to keep Rachel and Cornelius, Dinah's children, enslaved by his family, while Dinah roamed *free*. Ryan's lack of concern for Dinah's family and his willingness to rip asunder a Black family is no different from John Benger's actions in Ferryland. Both wills are characteristic of the wanton contempt the Black family structure has withstood. This happened on the plantations in the West Indies and throughout the United States and it happened in Newfoundland. Non-white family dismemberment continues today in Canada and the United States with the mass incarceration of people of colour.

Emily Davidson refers to Dinah's family separation as layered abolition. How could Dinah have been *free* in the city when her children were still enslaved? We do not know if Dinah's children were the result of consensual relationships or from forced intimacy with her owners.

We do not know if there was anyone else in the Ryan household made to help lighten Dinah's load, save her children, Rachel and Cornelius. It is likely, as the only domestic enslaved person to the Ryan family, Dinah reared eight children of varying ages, her own as well, and nurtured John Ryan and his wife. Twelve people, 13 if Dinah herself is included in the list of people she needed to care for. Dinah was accountable for the housework and likely the yard work, as no field slave is mentioned. The members of the Ryan household had unchecked control of her life and access to her body and her children. It boggles my mind that forceful subjugation of humans in any way could be considered *not bad*.

That John Ryan died after the abolition of slavery meant that he may have freed Dinah, Rachel, and Cornelius in 1834, if they were still alive. We do not know if he did. Historical records do not tell us more than a few crumbs about Dinah and her children.

Nelson points out that phrases such as "there were no Black people in Newfoundland" and "*if* there was slavery in Newfoundland, it was *not bad*" are attempts to minimize and make benign the history of the transatlantic slave trade in Newfoundland and Labrador. They silence Dinah's, and others like her, life, hardships, legacy, and connection to Newfoundland.

This frames the thought process that leads to the rampant forgetting and subsequent erasure of Black lives, Black stories, and Black struggles in Newfoundland history. Katherine, Dinah, Rachel, Cornelius, Sancho, Sarah, Nancy, Jack, Stephen. They all matter. They all deserved freedom.

Slave Ships
HB

"We're all awash in it," says Camille Turner. "You cannot look at any place and say, this is an innocent place." Newfoundland and Labrador is part of the Black Atlantic in many ways. Enslaved Black people passed through our ports aboard ships from many countries. Settlers of high status had enslaved Black people as indentured domestic workers.

Turner has brought more connections between Newfoundland and Labrador and enslaved Black Africans to the surface. In the 1700s and 1800s, many ships were built in Newfoundland. Enslaved Africans were moved around the Atlantic by ships. Those two statements collide in the Slave Voyages Database, a collection of research and data which scholars started working on in the 1960s and is now brought together in a website accessible to the public. It documents more than 36,000 voyages that transported enslaved Africans across the Atlantic against their will between 1514 and 1866.

Turner had a hunch. Considering that that database records tens of thousands of voyages across the Atlantic, what are the odds that Newfoundland would show up in there somewhere? Armed with her research on shipbuilding activity in the North Atlantic, Turner took a deep dive into the database.

Sure enough, Turner discovered some connections to what is now Atlantic Canada. "When I first encountered these ships, they were like an apparition to me. Like, what am I supposed to do with this?" Over the centuries, 40 ships used to transport slaves in the transatlantic slave trade were constructed in what is now Atlantic Canada. Nineteen of those ships were built in Newfoundland, from 1751 to 1792.

Then, Turner searched a database devoted to the intra-American slave trade. She has questions about 11 ships listed there. "There are also ships that are in that database and they're constructed in what they say is a plantation. So that plantation could be anywhere, including Newfoundland." In those small fishing settlements, especially from 1700 onward, shipbuilding had pride of place in Newfoundland and Labrador's history. The colony's economy was founded on the trades of the ocean, and ships were the workhorses that carried its goods. As with other lands where people made their living from the sea, Newfoundland was home to master shipbuilders and their workers who constructed the ships that were needed to do whatever work was at hand.

Ships and boats were made for everything from the inshore fishery to transatlantic trade.

The vessels sailed cargo around the Atlantic Ocean—to Europe, Africa, the United States, the Caribbean.

Goods were moved around on ships built in Newfoundland: cod, salt, rum, sugar, molasses. And people. Neil Kennedy, who has also combed through the Slave Voyages Database, spotted the 19 ships, all made in Newfoundland, all used to transport slaves, in the latter part of the 18th century: "This is not surprising because that was the peak of British involvement in the transatlantic slave trade, and Britain was the second largest participant after Portugal in the transatlantic slave trade."

The demand for ships to support British activities was constant. "Liverpool simply couldn't build ships fast enough to engage in the transatlantic slave trade. There are three other vessels Newfoundland built that were involved in what we call the intra-American Slave Trade, that is, transporting slaves between ports," explains Kennedy. "Mostly between Barbados, which was in decline as a sugar colony, then to Grenada, which was a relatively new sugar colony. In total, we have 22 Newfoundland-built vessels."

Most of these ships were small—40 to 160 tonnes—and easily adapted for multiple tasks. "Ships that were built as slavers were also merchant ships," Turner says. "They were easily transformed." They had shipwrights and carpenters on board. "When they would get to the African coast, they would build an extra deck to store human beings. When they had enough people, they would ship people one way and then they would ship goods another way. They [these ships] would be used for all kinds of different purposes. So, they were transforming all the time."

Kennedy is not surprised that ships used to transport slaves were built in Newfoundland. The use of enslaved Black people was so commonplace that slave labour was simply woven into all the other trades that were happening on the ocean at that time, such as the salt-cod trade, the sugar trade, the molasses trade, the people trade.

Camille Turner devoted her PhD research at Toronto's York University to the stories of the Newfoundland-built slave ships. Turner tells these stories through performance art. In 2019, her *Afronautic Research Lab* was part of the Bonavista Biennale. In it, she invited the public to explore the historical links between Newfoundland, shipbuilding, and the transatlantic slave trade. In a film that accompanies the project, Turner, a character from the future, dressed in white, walks on the top of a seaside cliff at Dungeon Provincial Park, near the Cape Bonavista lighthouse, where Giovanni Caboto supposedly made landfall in 1497. She carries a large rock to help tell a story.

A still image taken from "What the Ocean Remembers," a video from Camille Turner's *Afronautic Research Lab* installation (cinematographer and editor, Brian Ricks). Courtesy of the artist and the Bonavista Biennale. *Brian Ricks*

"Ships were built on these shores and, to ballast them, rocks were put in," Turner states. "They [the ships] would sail to the African shore. They would dump their rocks and then people would be put in. So those rocks are still on the African shore." Those rocks are from Newfoundland. "What we're living is produced by that past. And Newfoundland was very central, centrally located within the locus of this convergence of social, historical, and economic factions."

Turner considers how Newfoundland and Labrador's tourism marketing efforts show the province. Pristine, unspoiled coastlines and wilderness. "Look at Newfoundland and Labrador's tourism [industry] and the way that the province is presented. It's presented as an innocent space. It's not part of how this place is constructed to see itself. But there's so much more that's hidden."

The *Sarah*
HB

Camille Turner cannot stop thinking about the *Sarah*. Of the 19 ships made in Newfoundland in the Slave Voyages Database and the 11 others she flagged in the intra-American database, the *Sarah* had enough documentation for Turner to piece together its story. It was a 140-tonne multi-purpose ship built somewhere in Newfoundland in 1788 for merchant James Rogers of Bristol, England. Its construction would have been a large shipbuilding project. Some local residents would have cut trees for lumber, others were carpenters who put together the vessel, others caulked and made the ship seaworthy. Shipwrights, possibly from England or Ireland, may have been brought in to lead the operation.

The work in progress would have been an impressive sight and the talk of the town. I wonder why, here in Newfoundland and Labrador, we do not know more about these community shipbuilding projects.

In 1788, the *Sarah* made its maiden voyage from Newfoundland, eastward across the Atlantic Ocean, to Bristol, England, where it was put into service on the transatlantic trade routes. But before it left Bristol, more workers made modifications to jam as much human cargo into the hold of the *Sarah* as possible. Turner's research shows that breathing holes had been gouged into the sides of the *Sarah*. A lattice-like grated deck was added to let more air into the hull. Interior decks to store people were added.

These decks could have heights between 40 centimetres to 1 metre, enough to hold humans in sitting or crouched positions. Some of the enslaved Africans would not survive the *Sarah*'s voyages.

The *Sarah* made three voyages from England to the west coast of Africa to the Caribbean and back to England. Along the way, crew on the ship or carpenters in ports could modify the ship to accommodate whatever cargo needed to be carried—from sugar to cod to rum to humans. On its third voyage, on the final leg back to England, the *Sarah* sank.

In her research, Turner encountered this passage:

> The vessel arrived at Grand Bassa on the Windward Coast about 7 December and after "a Most tedious passage of 56 days" and reached its principal trading location at Bembia and the river Cameroon around 18 December. Its trade book shows that it purchased 256 slaves at the coast. These included 19 men, 12 women, 5 boys, and 5 girls bought at Bembia; 110 men, 46 women, 5 boys, and 7 girls bought at Cameroon, some of them supplied by the Nimble; and 22 men, 20 women, and 5 girls bought from William Blake, master of the Pearl (1790123) at Old Calabar. Its total purchase included, therefore, 151 men, 78 women, Io boys, and 17 girls. Some slaves may have died at the coast, for the vessel was said to have reached Barbados with only 142 slaves, having reportedly lost 80 in the crossing with "the flux and fever." It was recorded as importing 143 slaves at Jamaica, but the agent who sold them, John Fowler, noted that 141 were sold.[30]

---

30 David Richardson, ed., *Bristol, Africa and the Eighteenth-Century Slave Trade to America*. Vol. 4: The Final Years, 1770-1807 (Bristol Record Society Publications, Vol. 47, 1996), 157.

Humans, reduced to numbers, counted like goods, sold as easily as sacks of flour or barrels of molasses.

"You see what life was worth," Turner says. She found it challenging to wrap her head around the abstract way that record keepers documented the Black Africans that were captured, bought, transported, and sold. "The humanity of Africans could not be acknowledged at all. That's what allowed them [the traders] to do it."

Turner pushed through archive after archive, database after database. "How do I remember the people who were in that hold? How do I find these people?" She sought more clues on what became of the Newfoundland-built ships that had transported enslaved Black Africans in the 1700s.

The paper trail for slave ships is sparse, as it is for the other ships known to have been built in Newfoundland. Any documentation Turner did find was similar to the account of the *Sarah*, noting the numbers of crew and slaves on arrivals and departures and purchase prices and duties for the human cargo.

Based on that information, Turner thinks that it is likely that other ships built in Newfoundland that transported enslaved people would have similar tales to tell. The research and time she spent thinking about the people who were packed into these ships have taken their toll on her: "For me to survive that archive, I had to conjure a liberated future. Think of a time when these crimes of the past are not hidden anymore. What I do is I fill it with my own response."

Turner's response is through art. Her work is rooted in the concept that art can help others more effectively understand the unheard voices of Black people in the past, present, and into the future. From her research, Turner has constructed three video pieces called *Unmapped: An Afronautic Journey*. The videos have been used as part of installations in galleries across Canada and are available online on Turner's website. The first is part of her *Afronautic Research Lab*. Another video, *Nave*, intertwines three scenes—a church in Newfoundland overlooking the sea, a Black time traveller entering the church and performing a ritual, and a woman rising from water "to remind the African diaspora of the strength and resilience of ancestors who crossed the water on slave ships." Turner notes that when the nave of a church is upside down, it resembles the hold of a ship. A third video, *Sarah*, explores the experience of a Black researcher digging into the past while experiencing anti-Black violence in the present.

Turner's dedication of *Unmapped* states: "These artworks are dedicated to ancestors who survived the journey across the Atlantic to author a new world, to those of us who are their descendants still striving and surviving in the wake of slavery and to those whose bones lay on the bottom of the Atlantic."

Quieted Community Affairs
XMC

"The humanity of Africans was not allowed into the archives," Camille Turner says. It would have muddied their otherwise meticulous records.

I was first introduced to Turner's work about Newfoundland-built slave ships in 2019 at the Bonavista Biennale. In the Slave Voyages Database, Africans' essence, their personality traits, were not tabulated; the lives of millions of people were whittled down to tally marks and eventually a number on the internet. The counting of captured people for sale and the counting of people who died along the journey across the Middle Passage fill the database.

I thought I knew about Newfoundland's shipbuilding history. Thanks to Turner's work, I realized that I knew only of the celebrated histories that flood local lore and Newfoundland outport museums. Her work shows that the oral histories are incomplete.

Between 1750 and 1792, Newfoundland communities constructed vessels that were eventually used to capture and transport Africans to the New World. The slave ships were built by entire Newfoundland communities. That action forever ties the members of that community to the souls of every human being that boarded their ships. It took time to wrap my mind around the information presented in the Slave Voyages Database. Were they really referring to friendly Newfoundland, my new home?

By the 18th century, Newfoundland had a reputation for excellence in shipbuilding; Newfoundland shipbuilders played a key role in boat evolution, culminating in the development of the schooner. Prominent shipbuilding families in outports forged generations of builders with great impetus to propel the island's settlement. Family-run shipbuilding firms, such as Lester's in Trinity, constructed 10 to 12 vessels large enough for transatlantic voyages between the 1750s and early 1770s. Shipbuilders, their families, and businesses were invaluable to the development of culture and society during early settlement. When a community received a shipbuilding contract, it was a celebration. Everyone had work to do, a source of income a few degrees of separation from the almighty cod.

Many hands built these ships. The bonds and spirited camaraderie between co-workers as they chopped wood, made planks, and hammered. The skill needed to uphold the tradition of excellent boats made in Newfoundland. The passing of knowledge from generation to generation.

With such community involvement, I would expect that the intense process of making these large ships would have woven its way into the folklore of the island. How was this not the case? Oral traditions are strong in Newfoundland. Were the boat builders of Newfoundland just making boats to order, isolated from the atrocities of the economic system that aided them? But Newfoundland fishers delivered cod to the islands of the Caribbean where enslaved Africans were forced to labour. Was it shame and a desire to disassociate from such a terrible legacy? The questions are endless. Regardless of whatever answers I can conjure, the result is a deafening silence, and one on which Turner says that everything depends.

The 22 Newfoundland-built ships used in the intra-American and the transatlantic slave trade represent 22 opportunities for nurturing human contact but also the destroying of so many

Newfoundland-Built Ships Delivering Enslaved Africans to Jamaica

Name of Ship	Enslaved Africans Delivered
Tonyn	299
Sarah	140
Friendship	208
Sarah	190
Sarah	176
Roebuck	310
Greyhound	166
Antelope	396
Total Africans Delivered	**1,885**

Data gathered from Slave Voyages Database

Africans' humanity. In an era when ships were used to connect the world, those built in Newfoundland tore families, people, and souls apart.

The 22 ships in the database range in size, type, and ownership. Some were owned by men history remembers as slave traders, such as Sir James Laroche and James Rogers. In 1788, Britain issued the Slave Trade Act that regulated conditions aboard slave ships for the first time. Prior to this, large groups of enslaved Africans were crammed into ships regardless of the size, such as the 403 enslaved Africans captured from Bonny, New Calabar, and Bight of Biafra and Gulf of Guinea Islands and put on the Newfoundland-made 130-tonne *Antelope*, en route to Jamaica. Or the 100-tonne snauw, the *Roebuck*, that loaded 330 enslaved Africans from the Gold Coast and delivered them to Jamaica.

Newfoundland-built ships, such as the *Good Hope, Mary, Greyhound, General Wolfe, Tonyn, Betsey, Swallow, Morning Star, Sarah,* and the others mentioned in this chapter, made trips across the Atlantic with enslaved Africans for delivery in the New World. Over 6,000 enslaved Africans boarded Newfoundland-made ships; 579 of them died during the voyage across the Atlantic. The 200-tonne *Friends* shipwrecked in 1779 after 25 enslaved Africans had embarked. It was en route to Trinidad and Tobago from Cape Coast Castle. The enslaved perished with the ship. The *Ocean* was a 207-tonne ship that purchased 359 Africans in Bight of Biafra and Gulf of Guinea Islands, Cameroon, and Gabon. Thirty-one were lost upon disembarkation in Barbados in 1794.

Plaques commemorating those lost at the hands of Newfoundland communities are not displayed in front of City Hall. To this day, the 6,004 people that were taken from their homes and put on Newfoundland-made vessels remain an indistinguishable number on a tally sheet in a database. Like the *Maria*, a 50-tonne schooner that transported 80 Africans to be sold in Grenada in 1791, 74 of the 80 captured Africans on board the Newfoundland-built vessel were children. The *Torbay*, a 146-tonne ship, carried 245 captured Africans, 52 of which were children, little boys and girls. Now forgotten.

The souls that were lost on these ships were often tossed overboard, forgotten by those who etched history. They made no one any money in death. Plantation owners acquired more shiploads of newly captured Africans to ensure that sugar production did not cease. When boats sank, more slave ships were built so that the transportation and exploitation of human beings could continue. More communities built these vessels. More rocks were loaded, more people stolen—then forgotten. Stripping these enslaved Africans of their humanity, their stories, their choices ensured that nothing stopped the system of plantation slavery. These people worked, died, and were forgotten and erased as if their personhoods were only a crumbling abstraction.

For these despicable acts of stark anti-Blackness and erasure to end in Newfoundland, the reputation of the hardworking, humble and exploited settlers of Newfoundland must be connected to the lives of the forgotten who were forced on those ships off the coast of Cameroon, Old Calabar, Bonny, and those who disembarked in Barbados, Jamaica, and throughout the Caribbean. We must remember, as well, the 579 who died of dysentery, dehydration, scurvy, or other unhygienic conditions on these ships.

Turner has done the emotionally taxing work of starting the remembering and imagining of this aspect of Newfoundland culture. The financial gain of those in Newfoundland from the exploitation of a race of people goes beyond the almighty cod that fed the enslaved in the Caribbean, caught in and around Newfoundland waters.

I came to Newfoundland by airplane and chose to stay. My joy from living in Newfoundland now sits with more complicated feelings about this added information about Newfoundland Black history. When I sit in my living room in front of the heat of the firebox and speak with my mother, who lives in a different country, the woman who I yearn to be close to, I cannot help but think of all those people who boarded ships made on these shores and the relentess heat they were forced to work under for the rest of their lives. Because I am here, I can imagine: what if my ancestors were passengers on the *Sarah*? Among those who survived the journey across the Middle Passage on a Newfoundland-made ship? The shackles, cramped quarters, bodies pushed into other bodies, the terror, fecal matter, tiny air holes for breathing.

As Turner has said, "our Blackness, the individuality of Black people was not permitted to enter the record books." Captured Africans were forgettable tally marks to their captors and future enslavers. Let us think of those stolen innocent souls when we think of Newfoundland. Turner urges us all to remember the people in the hold.

Emancipation
XMC

Starting in the 1790s, some British people questioned the practice of slavery; this was mostly a matter of economics: as the sugar trade was being taken over by Brazil and Cuba, demand for goods produced by slave labour on British Caribbean plantations decreased. A handful of legal challenges against the practice was raised in British North America—now known as Canada. Owners of enslaved Black people were increasingly fearful of their human property; slave uprisings against their owners on plantations were common.

Yet, many merchants and businesspeople were opposed to ending slavery. Where else would they find all that free labour?

According to Dale Jarvis, Newfoundland became an argument for pro-slavery advocates: "There are documents from the early 1800s that showed that one of the excuses or reasons that the pro-slavery lobby maintained was, 'Well, if we get rid of the Atlantic slave trade, what's going to happen to all those Newfoundlanders who are selling codfish and all those Newfoundlanders who work as sailors?'" says Jarvis. "And it was estimated, you know, that 'if we get rid of slavery, then Newfoundland will be a problem because how are we going to continue to support that colony?' We were actually used as an excuse to perpetuate that system."

Concerns about Newfoundland did not stop slavery abolitionists. In 1833, Britain passed the Slavery Abolition Act. It took effect on August 1, 1834, making it illegal for British citizens to own another human being. That started the process of disassembling large-scale plantation slavery in the British colonies in the Caribbean and emancipating enslaved Black people all over the British empire.

Over the next few decades, the entire Atlantic world—Western Europe, the Americas, and West Africa—ended the centuries-old practice of enslaving Black people. What happened to all the Black people who had passed through Newfoundland harbours and landed on Newfoundland shores?

According to W. Jeffrey Bolster, Black men continued to work aboard ships at sea, although for paltry wages. They were also pushed into lower-ranking jobs with lower wages, with white sailors taking the higher-paid, higher-skilled jobs at sea. After slavery was abolished, Black men had options for low-paying but safer jobs on land. By the late 1800s, far fewer Black sailors were found aboard American vessels.[31]

What about the enslaved Black domestic workers in Newfoundland? As Emily Davidson told us, even if they were freed, where could they go? They had very few resources, they were of low status, and their options were limited.

"I always feel these things are in our unconscious mind," Afua Cooper says. "Maybe just below the level of our consciousness until something happens."

---

31   Bolster, *Black Jacks*, 176.

Jamaica's Journey: Abolition to Independence
HB

While the British parliament outlawed the transportation of enslaved people from Africa to Jamaica in 1808, emancipation was not granted to enslaved Africans in Jamaica until 1834. Even then, this was no gift of freedom. Instead, after the so-called emancipation, enslaved Africans were forced into a period of apprenticeship. Over the next four years, they were made to work, uncompensated, for their former masters. Full freedom was not offered to enslaved Africans in Jamaica until 1838. Streets were filled as many gathered to hear the words of the Emancipation Declaration, ostensibly ending apprenticeship. Three decades after the alleged abolition of slavery.

Marred by continuous revolts and rebellions, the transatlantic slave trade lasted for over 300 years in Jamaica. The 1838 abolition of the system of bondage there led to the implosion of the plantation system but not the system of oligarchy that permeated the island. The former enslaved people did not want to work for their former masters and the conditions for poor Africans were still worse than for the white people on the island. The will of the Black majority was wholly ignored. In 1865, tensions between Blacks and whites were high, soaring unemployment ravaged the island, the Jamaican people were heavily taxed, and a drought culminated in the Morant Bay Rebellion.

Paul Bogle and his supporters stormed the sitting Morant Bay Courthouse, armed with machetes and stones, protesting widespread poverty and racial injustice. Black Jamaicans were still barred from voting. After the Jamaican militia opened fire, killing protestors, pandemonium ensued. More than 20 people died. Over the next two days, Bogle and his supporters took control of the parish. The uprising was viciously quashed by the authorities. The government militia killed over 400 Black people, including women and children, and hundreds more, including Bogle, were arrested. All the rebellion leaders were hanged, including Bogle and wealthy politician George William Gordon, both of whom are now national heroes. The cruel and unilateral behaviour of British governor Edward John Eyre led to the fall of the Jamaican Assembly and ushered in a new era of Crown colony government in 1866.

Jamaica benefitted from social, constitutional, and economic advancement in the subsequent years. Because it was a sovereign state, access to social services, education, and health care improved. In 1872, Kingston became its official political capital. The United Negro Improvement Association (UNIA) was launched in Jamaica in 1914 by Jamaican Black nationalist, activist, and politician Marcus Garvey. He fostered the international awareness of the right of the Black race to coexist as equals with the other humans in the rest of the world. Garvey, the first named national hero of Jamaica, is credited with awakening Black pride and consciousness in millions of Black people in Africa and throughout the diaspora.

The Great Depression of the 1930s ushered in another calamity. Black people were still dissatisfied with the slow pace of political advancement. In 1938, rioting and violence erupted. As a result of the disturbances, the island's two major political parties were formed: the Jamaica Labour Party (JLP) led by Alexander Bustamante in 1943 and the People's National Party (PNP) led by Norman Manley in 1938. Two labour unions were also created: the Bustamante Industrial Trade Union (BITU) associated with the JLP, while the National

Worker's union was linked to the PNP. Bustamante and Manley, both now national heroes, were instrumental in the move toward Jamaican self-governance. On November 20, 1944, England granted Jamaica universal suffrage. The election of December 1944 was the first on the island under universal suffrage. Jamaica became the third British state, behind New Zealand and England, to have an election under universal suffrage. Before, voting was restricted to wealthy men who owned property. The new system allowed all adults to vote, regardless of race, sex, or financial status. It caused a windfall of self-governance throughout the British West Indies. Jamaica was granted its independence from England on August 6, 1962.

What Now?
HB

When I was in grade school in the 1970s and 1980s, our textbooks and teachers told us that Newfoundland was founded by people who looked like me—pale-skinned, blue-eyed, and of English and Irish descent. Despite the harsh conditions, the relentless work, the grinding poverty, these hardy, white souls were determined to stick it out here. Our friendly, welcoming ways, creativity, and good humour gave us the strength to keep going through hard times. These stories, told by historians and storytellers, are ingrained in Newfoundland and Labrador culture. Scores of books, artworks, films, songs, and monuments attest to this version of Newfoundland and Labrador.

This is only part of our history and these are only some of our stories.

Black people were in Newfoundland, and on the coast of Labrador, on a regular basis for hundreds of years. Most of the time, they were here against their will. They were enslaved.

Newfoundland was a key part of the Atlantic triangular trade, an economic system that is the reason people came to live in Newfoundland in the first place. The work that made the triangular trade go round, for European nations to grow richer, and for colonization to happen in North and South America, could not have happened without the labour and lives of enslaved Black people.

The first time I recall learning about Black people in Newfoundland and Labrador history is in the context of World War II, as they were members of the American military. The island of

Newfoundland, because of its strategic spot in the North Atlantic, became a site for several American military bases.

Then there is the story of Black American serviceman Lanier Phillips, who was rescued from the shipwreck of the USS *Truxton* in 1942 in the waters off Newfoundland's Burin Peninsula by the people of the nearby town of St. Lawrence. Phillips was so moved by the kindness shown to him by the people of St. Lawrence that, after his rescue, he was inspired to become a civil rights activist and became the first Black sonar technician in the American Navy.

But what about all the Black people that would have passed through, or lived, in Newfoundland between Emancipation and World War II? What about Newfoundland's contribution to the triangular trade? What about Black people who may not have been treated as kindly as Lanier Phillips was?

As Dale Jarvis has said, "It's hard for people to wrap their heads around the fact that the stories that we have always been told aren't necessarily true and that we aren't the heroes of our own stories all the time."

What do the lives of Black people who were in Newfoundland hundreds of years ago have to do with Xaiver, a Black man from Jamaica, now living in Newfoundland, or me, a white woman, living in Newfoundland, with deep ancestral roots here?

As Camille Turner asks us to consider: "What do we do with all this information?"

The Cod Endures
HB

The transatlantic slave trade may have ended in the mid-1800s, but the circulation of goods around the Atlantic Ocean continued. From Europe to North America, down to the Caribbean and South America, back to Europe and west Africa, the goods kept flowing. Cod was always swimming in the Atlantic Ocean's triangular trade. On every shore touched by the Atlantic Ocean, people ate cod. It was cheap, portable, durable, and familiar.

From *bacalhau a bras* in Portugal, to *brandade de morue* in France, to ackee and salt fish in Jamaica, to fish and brewis in Newfoundland, rich or poor, Black or white, free or enslaved, cod filled many bellies.

Newfoundland fishers caught cod, salted it, and sold it to local merchants who then sold it to European, American, and Caribbean buyers. Newfoundland trading companies regularly ran ships back and forth between Newfoundland and the Caribbean. European, American, and Caribbean ships continued to come to Newfoundland to fish their own cod. Portuguese fishing boats, known as the White Fleet, and their crews, became especially familiar visitors to St. John's and other fishing ports in Newfoundland through most of the 20th century.

Did anyone on this cold, rocky North Atlantic island eat anything else but cod? Surely everyone needed variety in their diets. Anything that Newfoundlanders could not fish, hunt, grow, or forage had to be imported.

In exchange for cod, Newfoundland received salt and port wine from Portugal and Spain, tobacco from the United States, and molasses, rum, sugar, and more salt from the Caribbean.

In Newfoundland and Labrador, until the mid-20th century, salt cod served as a de facto currency. Most people, especially those who lived in rural Newfoundland and made their living from the ocean, were poor. Fishers brought salt cod to merchants. The merchants took the cod and gave the fishers dry goods such as fabric, nails, and household supplies. They also gave fishers pantry staples: tea, flour, and molasses. Very little, if any, cash was ever exchanged. Most of the time, fishers received barely enough supplies to get them and their families through the never-ending winters.

Molasses, which came from the Caribbean, was as much of a staple in Newfoundland pantries as cod. It sweetened everything from tea to puddings to thick slices of warm homemade bread.

Today, the idea of a traditional Newfoundland and Labrador meal might be one taken in a cozy kitchen in a small fishing outport. A kindly grandmother, often called Nan, prepares a plate of salt cod, brewis (hard bread), and scruncheons (cubes of fried pork fat). For dessert, Nan makes molasses buns, and you wash those warm buns down with a cup of strong tea. If Nan is feeling naughty, she might add a slug of rum to that tea. A simple but tasty and stick-to-your-ribs kind of meal. Now you are ready for a nap on the daybed by the woodstove. Unless you start to think about the darker, more complicated flavours in that meal.

Think about all the hands—white and Black, Newfoundland and Caribbean—that are joined by fish, rum, and molasses. The poor hands, the enslaved hands, the hands working in dangerous environments. Hands that hauled nets of codfish and salted them. Hands that cut the sugar cane and stirred the vats of molasses. Hands that were all part of an economic system that was built on enslaved labour.

The Thing about Fish
HB

Growing up in St. John's in the 1970s and 1980s in a family that has roots in Newfoundland and Labrador stretching back generations, I ate a lot of fish. When I say fish, I mean cod. Anything else—capelin, salmon, halibut—well, they are not fish. They are capelin, salmon, halibut.

Fresh fish, a.k.a. cod, is easy to find around Newfoundland and Labrador for most of the year. In the summer and fall, it is pulled straight from the ocean, and it freezes well.

In my family, we prized the buttery, flaky flesh and delicate taste of fresh fish. At home, my grandmother, who lived with us, boiled or pan-fried it and served it with boiled potatoes and scruncheons and homemade pickles or homemade bottled beets for condiments.

Salt fish, however, was always available for backup. Salt fish has stood the test of time, and the test of modern freezers, and occasionally showed up on our family menu. Salt fish was used to make the traditional Newfoundland dish of fish and brewis. Fish and brewis goes back to the decades, even centuries, before Newfoundland and Labrador was a province of Canada, a time before refrigeration, a time when the only vegetables were those that you grew, and non-perishable food items available from the local merchant were very basic.

At our house, my grandmother soaked salt fish in fresh water for a few hours, maybe overnight. At the same time, she soaked hard bread, also known as hard tack, another indestructible food item that is soaked in water and reconstituted. Fishers took hard bread with them for long stints at sea. The local commercial brand, Purity Hard Bread, comes in small, fist-shaped cakes in bright red and yellow bags. Our traditional Newfoundland palate tends to favour durable ingredients. After everything was softened and rehydrated, my grandmother boiled the fish, hard bread, and locally grown potatoes in the same pot.

There are various ways to top this warm, slightly salty, off-white combination of fish, hard tack, and potatoes. Some serve it with drawn butter, a sauce similar to a French roux. We scattered scruncheons on the fish and potatoes, and to liven up the bland taste of brewis, we sprinkled sugar on it, or maybe molasses. It was tasty and filling, a salty and sweet meal.

If we had any leftovers, my grandmother made fish cakes. The salt fish and potatoes were mashed together, combined with minced onion and savoury and patted into hockey-puck-sized fish cakes. Dredged in flour and pan-fried. Delicious.

Cod was still king of the Newfoundland and Labrador supper table until the early 1990s. Then its large-scale commercial cod fishery, which had thrived for 500 years, collapsed. Too many fish were being taken out of the sea to sustain a healthy population. The government moratorium on codfishing caused economic and social turmoil, but that is a story for another time. A generation has passed now, without the reign of King Cod.

If you know where to look, you can still get a good feed of fish in Newfoundland and Labrador. Nowadays, most people find their "fish" through small-scale vendors, or they catch it themselves in the small amounts the government allows for personal use. Restaurants and fish and chip shops have their own arrangements with local purveyors.

In my own family, cod, fresh or salted, does not show up as often as it once did on our dinner menu. Salt fish is now most often cooked by older people at home, although, these days, more and more restaurants offer it for tourists.

Supermarket chains do not carry much local cod. Small fresh or salted portions might be packaged on foam trays, but that is about it. Most locally caught fish, including cod, is exported. Cod is now an occasional treat for me.

Imagine my surprise when, in 2022, I walked into a modern supermarket in a small town on the coast of Portugal and saw a display of *bacalhau*—the big, flat salt fish of my childhood. Bacalhau is as common a grocery-store staple in southwestern Europe as milk and bananas. I saw restaurant menus with entire sections of bacalhau dishes. It comes from the North Sea these days. In many lands that border on the Atlantic Ocean, people still love salt fish. In these places, cod is still king.

Bacalhau of southwestern Europe. Salt fish of the Caribbean. Stockfish of West Africa. In each place, on each continent, salt fish, a.k.a. salted cod, is both a throwback to the days before modern refrigeration and the industrial food supply chain and a regular item to buy for supper.

Some dishes are bland, others are fiery with spices. Endless variations on salt-fish cakes or fritters. Salt fish makes people of many colours, cultures, creeds, and stations in life think of their grandmothers.

What is *with* the salt cod? What happens when we drop anchor on a map—and circle all the places where people love to eat salt fish? We are all points on the centuries-old triangular trade and transatlantic slave-trade routes.

A display of salt cod for sale in a modern supermarket in Tavira, Portugal. *Heather Barrett*

Kevin Toope's Salt Fish
HB

Not all salt fish is alike. It comes in different grades. In Newfoundland in the past, these have been Premium Grade, Madeira Grade, and West Indies or Jamaica Grade. If you want to figure out the differences, you need to talk to Kevin Toope. Toope has been making salt fish as long as he can remember.

"The first colour photograph ever taken of me is with me and my mother, on the beach drying salt cod." Toope grew up in Trinity, on Newfoundland's Bonavista Peninsula, which for centuries was a hub for the English migratory and year-round fishery and home to shipbuilders and other tradespeople. These days, Trinity is one of the busiest tourist destinations in the province, a go-to place for theatre, whale watching, and fine local dining. During the tourist season, Toope operates a busy walking-tour business, during which he tells people from all over the world about Trinity's long and proud fishing heritage. He also throws Newfoundland history and his own family history into his guided rambles around the town. Toope will tell you everything you did not realize you needed to know about cod.

Toope grew up in a traditional fishing family. His father was a cod fisher and his mother salted and dried cod on the shore. The Toopes then sold their catch to local Newfoundland merchants, who then sold it to customers in the Caribbean or Europe. Toope moved to St. John's to attend university, and then he stayed in the city for a long career as a teacher. All the while, he led another

Salt cod is laid out to dry on a traditional fish flake in Trinity. *Kevin Toope*

life as a traditional Newfoundland bayman. When he taught me high school chemistry in the 1980s, he went home to Trinity in the summers to fish with his father and to "make fish" with his mother. He spends winters in St. John's and the rest of the year in Trinity. Toope still fishes, salts, and dries his own cod. His legendary salt cod is the most popular and sought-after item in the Trinity Historical Society's fundraising auction.

Jamaica Grade salt fish? Toope knows all about it.

But first, he walks us through the process of preserving cod, starting in the Atlantic Ocean.

Toope and his father steamed out of Trinity harbour in a small open fishing boat, the kind Newfoundland fishers had used for centuries. They caught each cod individually by hook and line or in small batches in cod traps. That took several hours, with their catch piling up on the bottom of the boat. In the afternoon, they headed back to shore in Trinity. That is when the next phase of the fisher's work started—cleaning the fish.

"You would take a sharp knife, cut the throat, take the head off, clean out the guts, split the fish all the way to the tail. Then wash the fish with salt water to clean it," Toope says. Once the fish is cleaned and washed, it is ready to be salted. "Salt was really important. High-quality salt was evaporated from salt water, and lower quality was rock salt, which was mined."

A light salt involved stacking layers of salt and split and cleaned fish. After five or six days, the weight of the stack pressed out excess moisture. Then, if weather conditions were optimal, the fish were ready for drying. Another method, known as a heavier salt, involved splitting and cleaning the fish, then putting it in a container of salt to pickle it. Then the fish was ready to be dried.

For crews fishing on the Labrador or on the Grand Banks and spending multiple days at sea, the fish was put in salt in the ships' holds. When the crew reached land, the fish was washed and dried. Then, the split, flattened, and salted fish were laid out in the open air, on rocky beaches, to dry. Ideal drying weather was windy, dry, not too hot or sunny. Too much sun or heat, and the fish burned or cooked.

The best-quality salt cod, Toope continues, is made in the fall, when the weather is cooler, drier, and windy. That was when fishers made salt fish for their own consumption, after they had fulfilled their obligations to merchants and other buyers. They saved the best salt cod for themselves.

Toope rattles all this off in his practiced tour-guide voice. Salt fish is complicated. "Doing all of this took a fair bit of skill, and also a bit of luck. Not all fishermen were equally skilled in their salt fish production, and not all weather worked in their favour."

However, the fish could become maggoty, get salt burn, or be "dun," that is, get a fungal infection which turned the salt and the fish pink. As salt cod became ready for market, merchants sent schooners to collect it. A culler on board each schooner graded the fish according to quality. Different markets wanted different salt fish. Some wanted fish with white flesh. Others preferred a yellowish cast. Very thin salt fish, the cheaper fish, was sent to the Caribbean.

Salt fish was graded this way until the 1980s. Toope still has documents from his father which describe the various grades of fish and the prices they commanded. By then, the poorest quality fish was called "cullage," but everyone knew that that meant "Jamaica Grade." Still, no one, including Toope, thought about the origin of the term "Jamaica Grade." It was just the name. The idea that Jamaica Grade came from the cheapest form of protein to feed enslaved Black people in that country was nowhere in the average Newfoundland fisher's field of knowledge.

Still, ties between Trinity and the Caribbean, where Black people, in the 1700s and early 1800s, were enslaved, and generations of their descendants, were strong. "There were several local merchants in Trinity, such as Ben Lester, who had schooners with local crews who would go to the Caribbean," Toope says.

Toope emailed us another curious piece of information: a burial record from one of Trinity's churches: "The burial record says, 'April 5, 1804—Interred Don Pedro Classisso, one of Genl Hene's? band of musicians, a native of Martinique.' This is from a typed transcription of the original hand-written burial records. I'm assuming the transcriber couldn't pick out the general's surname. It may be Henesy's or Henry's."

A musician from Martinique, aboard a vessel commanded by a General Henesy or a General Henry, died and was buried in Trinity in 1804. Toope speculates that he could have been of African or perhaps Spanish or Portuguese descent. That musician, a man of colour from aboard a ship, was buried in Trinity around the same time that W.H. was buried in L'Anse au Loup.

What was a group of musicians from Martinique doing on a ship in or near Trinity in 1804? Were they there for a concert? Was Trinity a stop on the way to somewhere else? Were they enslaved or were they free? How many more unnamed Black people are buried in cemeteries in small communities scattered around the coasts of Newfoundland and Labrador?

Newfoundland did not exist in its own fogbound, pale English Irish world. It was a port of call in the Black Atlantic.

Colonial Foodways Today
XMC

Even though the days of the transatlantic slave trade have long passed, oppressive colonialism persists in society today. One such way is in our food. Kevin Toope talks about the thin fish sent down to the West Indies. Of how this fish would become even thinner by the time it was unloaded on the shores of Caribbean islands after travelling across the Atlantic Ocean. The cullage. Maggoty fish. Any fish with a blemish, any fish the culler wanted to pay less money for. In 2023, while the salt fish delivered to islands such as Jamaica is no longer filled with maggots, and comes from varying locations, it remains a lesser grade than that sent to European markets and sold in stores in Newfoundland.

Lesser-grade fish became a staple in the Jamaican diet as a direct result of slavery and colonialism. Since the days of the transatlantic slave trade to the 20th century, Newfoundland fishers have delivered countless tonnes of codfish to the Caribbean islands. Although Jamaica received large deliveries of salt fish, such as 325 tonnes in 1948, fishers made less money because of its poor quality. Like millions of Jamaicans before me, I grew up on lesser-grade salt fish even as the 21st century dawned, hundreds of years after the abolition of the transatlantic slave trade.

Why does this remain the case? It is unconscionable that many Jamaicans remain ignorant of the juicy, flaky version of salt fish. After Jamaica gained its independence from the British, ackee and salt fish became the national dish. I am confident my people would enjoy having prime or choice pieces of salt fish with their ackee.

I do not suggest changing the things that make Newfoundlanders proud of their history; I ask that we question certain things more critically. The screech-in, for example. To be an "honourary" Newfoundlander, one is baptized by a shot of Screech, bastardized Jamaican rum. The by-product of sugar production. But why and how did this liquid become the representative waters of the Newfoundlander? Why is this never mentioned in league with the frivolities?

Newfoundland culture developed amid the height of slavery and colonialism and has only strengthened in its traditions over the centuries. The celebrated ingredients, the spirits, and the struggles glue Newfoundlanders and Labradorians together. However, these same ingredients, spirits, and struggles tether Newfoundland to Jamaica and islands like it, from their time as countries run by the exploited labour of enslaved Africans to the present.

These bonds make people feel at home when they first arrive in Newfoundland. When I learned that people in Newfoundland liked salt fish, my heart soared. I was not expecting to find a cultural affinity for salt-cured protein outside of Jamaica. At Christmas time, I was given dark rum fruitcake. While it was not as boozy as it is back home, it was a welcome surprise to learn of another part of Jamaican culture in Newfoundland. It is hard not to think fondly of patois when I listen to Newfoundlanders speak their own elaborate variation of English.

Our memories may implicate us in the systems of colonialism that we wish to decry.[32] It is okay to sit with that discomfort instead of forgetting. It is with continued discussion of these issues and histories, and through asking the uncomfortable and difficult

---

32   Snooks and Boon, "Salt Fish and Molasses," 237.

questions, that we begin to unravel the grip colonialism and racist institutions have had on our entire lives, and a change can come. There is tremendous value in knowing more "truths" about ourselves and our past.

Heather Bakes
HB

Xaiver and I first bonded over our love of baking. He bakes professionally from time to time, and I am strictly a home baker. Sometimes I follow recipes from books, but my go-tos are tried and true recipes passed down through generations of my family. I like hearty, lightly sweetened treats such as muffins, buns, loaves, and biscuits made from the British tradition of baking. Most of those recipes call for locally grown ingredients—blueberries, partridgeberries, or rhubarb—or those close at hand in most grocery stores—flour, sugar, butter, eggs, cocoa powder, molasses, and coconut.

My grandmother's ginger-molasses cookie recipe is a hit, and somewhere I have handwritten directions for the classic Newfoundland snowball cookie, a small ball of cocoa, rolled oats, and canned evaporated milk, rolled in coconut.

The ingredients called for in these recipes have always been readily available at my local supermarket and were obviously available to Newfoundland bakers for generations, since they are critical to these old recipes.

Molasses is on the supermarket shelf, in everything from 250-millilitre cartons to 5-kilogram containers. Before the advent of the modern grocery store, molasses was available from merchant shops in 88-gallon puncheons, or wooden barrels, shipped from Jamaica. Kevin Toope can remember, as a youngster, being sent to the local shop in Trinity with a glass jar to be filled with molasses for his mother.

In addition to molasses being a staple in baking, Newfoundlanders and Labradorians use it as a condiment to spread on hot, fresh bread and to pour over everything from hot cereal to fish and brewis and molasses baked beans. And then there is the non-culinary use of molasses. "My grandfather used molasses as a cure," Toope recalls. "A teaspoon of kerosene oil and a teaspoon of molasses to cure a sore throat."

Coconut. That is what we call dried, shredded coconut that comes in small bags of coarse, white flakes. Coconut is a key ingredient in the classic Newfoundland snowball, and a sweet, textured addition to bar cookies. I never thought of *coconut* as having any relationship to *a* coconut. I never saw an actual coconut until well into adulthood.

Rum. To make a dark Christmas fruitcake, you need rum. Next door to my neighbourhood supermarket is a large Newfoundland Liquor Corporation store with an entire wall of rum: light rum, dark rum, amber rum, spiced rum. And a dark Jamaican rum called Newfoundland Screech.

A dark fruitcake, to be consumed at Christmas time, was made in advance and soaked in rum to preserve it. Rum balls, rolled in dried coconut, a variation on the Newfoundland snowball, are also a Christmas treat. Rum-raisin ice cream was a popular local flavour year-round. Bars on the George Street entertainment strip in downtown St. John's advertise specials on "dark and dirties"—dark rum and Coca Cola.

Like most people I know, I never stopped to consider why rum and molasses were so readily available in Newfoundland and Labrador. I also did not realize, until going to university in Ontario in the early 1990s, that these items were not staples in the mainland Canadian diet. Molasses instead of maple syrup on pancakes? Why drink rum when you could drink whiskey?

I had never thought about the Caribbean exports found on Newfoundland grocery shelves, because they were always there. I had never thought about why you could always find molasses, rum, and dried coconut and why those ingredients were always part of traditional Newfoundland recipes. It never occurred to me to link those pantry staples to the triangular trade, the transatlantic slave trade, and Newfoundland and Labrador.

I had never stopped to think about the hands that made these products for Newfoundlanders and Labradorians and about the raw materials that were needed to make them. I never thought about the centuries in which enslaved people worked in dangerous conditions to provide these staples to my northerly island. I never thought about sugar cane. I had never *seen* sugar cane. And why was an extremely processed by-product of the tropical coconut so popular?

I just made ginger-molasses cookies.

M'lasses
XMC

Newfoundland has afforded me the opportunity to lead many lives. One of the sweetest of those lives involved baking in some of the cafés in St. John's. I have weighed out countless kilograms of flour, butter, and sugar, all par for the course in any bakery. Another ingredient that was weighed prominently, to my surprise, was molasses.

My memories of molasses stem from childhood. I remember sitting on an overturned white bucket in our skinny rectangular kitchen. My grandmother stood by the sink in the corner, cutting thick slices of fresh, buttery, hard dough bread. The smell of bubbling braising meat everywhere. Her snack before the main course made complete by the brown jar on the cracked blue countertop. Inside the brown jar was her m'lasses. Thick, almost black, goop. The stickiest goop you have ever seen. Sometimes it felt like you got sticky just by looking at that brown jar. Finding childhood moments at work in Newfoundland was always comforting and jarring. Especially if in the dead of winter, when time moves as quickly as molasses rolling uphill.

Granny's m'lasses smelled like hardship and it tasted like it too. She loved its tangy, sharp notes; I opted to cover my own slice of fresh, warm, hard dough bread with condensed milk. We would cheer and devour a few slices before my mother was aware of our antics in the kitchen.

When I worked in bakeries, molasses became integral to my job. My memories are associated with how long a batch of molasses-raisin bread takes to bake: 16 minutes in a convection oven at 315°F. Molasses instead of sugar in pound cakes and madeleines, a must try, if I do say so myself. The ginger-molasses cookies baked in a year: countless. The potent dark brown liquid can overpower any recipe, caution always required when measuring. My relationship with m'lasses is ever evolving. I do not work in kitchens anymore but am still weighed down by overbearing, sticky molasses. The childhood version of myself would turn his head and stick out his tongue if he saw the white box covered in brown stains in my cupboard. A box that is often reached for when I yearn for ginger-molasses cookies or raisin bread. My time in Newfoundland has stirred within me various feelings toward molasses. I wish my grandmother were still alive so that we could share a slice of thick white bread slathered in molasses. I wish I could tell her that I live somewhere that has embraced molasses and kept its relevance alive for all these years so that I could have access to it.

It was not easy for me to embrace Newfoundland's unending love for molasses. As I wash its stickiness off my hands and return it to the cupboard, I think of the enslaved Africans who worked the sugar plantations. In Jamaica, if an enslaved person tried to run away and was caught, the master whipped them, then rubbed salt, pepper, and lime into their wounds for added punishment—to pickle the runaway. The pickling of the enslaved happened at the same time as those in Newfoundland added molasses to buns to make them tastier.

It was the African that brought molasses to Newfoundland. Molasses was a cheap food source. Another gift from the Age of Sugar; cheaper than honey, with nutritional value, it contains calcium, iron, copper, magnesium, other minerals and is a source of vitamins B and E. Diane Tye talks about the diverse uses of molasses, from sweetener to medicine to the sustenance of the working class who depended on the sugars from molasses as a cheap energy source.[33]

As I dug into how molasses became entrenched in Newfoundland culture, I knew the results would be as unpleasant as I had considered the taste of molasses as a child. But there is some sweetness in knowing that our pasts and our presents connect in so many surprising ways. The burns endured from the bubbling, boiling molasses splashes and the limbs lost as the sugar cane is ground into juice should not be forgotten. Those hardships along with the sweetness of a 100-year-old recipe covered in brown sticky fingerprints are the embodied testimonies needed to better understand the ongoing legacies of colonialism and slavery—which are intimately woven into most of our own histories.

When we think of molasses, when we eat it and pass down recipes to the next generations, it is worth passing down how the molasses came to be held in such high regard in their lives. That is something I must also think about each time I interact with molasses. After over a decade on this rock, I now crave molasses more.

Molasses is as much a part of the culture of Newfoundland as it is of Jamaica and that is worth discussion and celebration. The sticky stuff that binds us over oceans, generations, and time is still as culturally potent as ever.

---

[33] Diane Tye, "A Poor Man's Meal: Molasses in Atlantic Canada," *Food, Culture and Society* 11, no. 3 (2015): 335-53.

Foodways and Memories
XMC

Donna Norvey is an expert baker with ties to Lawn on Newfoundland's Burin Peninsula. She has as many fond memories of molasses as I do. Norvey grew up in Michigan in the United States. In the early 1960s, her mother hitchhiked from Lawn to St. John's to become a maid for a judge. She met Norvey's father, a United States Navy officer, while he was on his night off in St. John's. The two fell in love and were married. The couple left Newfoundland in 1961 and the rest is history. Now a folklorist living in Newfoundland, Norvey believes that knowing the connections between molasses, Newfoundland, Jamaica, and her family adds a richer dimension to her memories and her own family history. In her work, Norvey strives to tell everyone's stories through the collection of customs, household artifacts, and lores highlighting the countless ways our histories and practices are linked.

Norvey and I sat down in the community room of the Torbay History House and Museum, where she works, to talk about how food connects people across time and space. After all, we all need to eat. We discussed how food, customs, and ingredients link us to the past. Particularly, what does this mean for us in the present and the stories we were told? If more complete histories are recorded, will this affect how and what stories we choose to tell in the future?

As a child in the US, Norvey recalls that "molasses on toast was a popular after school snack." Generous servings of Crosby's molasses on thick slices of her mother's homemade white bread made going to school worthwhile. The Crosby's carton was always sticky, and if it was too cold in the house, "we had to warm it up. It was an extra special treat when there was molasses-raisin bread to sample." As Norvey recognizes now, the presence of that snack may have stemmed from her mother's homesickness for Newfoundland. After all, "it was the same molasses-raisin bread that my mother used to make when she was a child living in Newfoundland."

Norvey first came to Newfoundland at age nine on a summer camping trip. She recalls getting off the overnight ferry in Argentia and driving to Lawn. Her mother was one of 15 children. The connection to family was instant and extensive: "That summer, there were always 10 kids in the house. Four kids and six cousins. Everyone with sticky fingers chewing on bread." Bread slathered in molasses.

This white bread she watched her Aunt Kate bake without a care for any metrics of measurement. The recipe is as follows:

- a bowl of bread and roll flour, quantity based on how much bread to be made
- a sprinkle of yeast on top of the flour
- one swipe of butter
- one pinch of salt
- coffee cup of milk
- some water

The milk was the only consistent measure.

In the US, Norvey tried her hand at nursing, since her sister was a nurse in Michigan, but she soon realized that her calling was to nourish the body through food. She enrolled in a two-year culinary arts program. Upon graduation, she found herself at the prestigious

McKenna Island Hotel. Eventually Norvey became the baker at the hotel, but something was missing.

In 2012, Norvey visited Newfoundland for a Come Home Year, a two-week celebration in St. John's including a screech-in and a dance, but more importantly, a molasses and food day. It was unusual to see molasses highlighted. Norvey had always loved molasses bread and molasses spread on bread. In culinary school, and generally in American culture, "molasses goes into things," Norvey explains. "Ginger cookies, gingerbread houses, spice cake. It was the 'flavour' element. It was not used by itself. It is never the star of the show like it is in Newfoundland."

Norvey knew that she needed a job in Newfoundland to make her dream possible. In 2014, she landed the position as the head cake, cookies, and pastry baker at Rocket Bakery in St. John's.

As she was immersed in the world of the Rocket Bakery, Norvey realized that molasses was everywhere in Newfoundland. "It was impossible to keep the ginger-molasses cookies on the shelf. We went through about at least a gallon of molasses or more per week. We made a multigrain bread sweetened with molasses [and] molasses-raisin bread, ginger-molasses cookies, gingerbreads at Christmas."

Nowadays, Norvey spends very little time in a production-style kitchen. But when she is sad and needs a dose of good memories, she breaks out the sticky tub of molasses from the back of her cupboard. As the viscous liquid coats a slice of thick toast, she cannot help but smile and think of her mother.

Her mother was born in 1939. The Depression left her family, like many others, with barely two pennies to rub together. "White sugar was very expensive, but she could get a barrel of molasses or fill a container with a smaller quantity to take home."

Through her studies, and from the public work of some of the experts interviewed for this book, Norvey has become aware of the connections between molasses, Newfoundland, Jamaica, and the transatlantic slave trade. While this added information about Newfoundland's involvement in this slave trade is shrouded in darkness, colonialism, and the bitterness of slavery, it has not altered Norvey's love and respect for her mother and the rest of her Newfoundland family.

There has been a shift, however, in how she views her family's history and memories of her mother. Now her memories of molasses make her think about the slave trade, as well as her family. She recognizes that shame may have played a part in the reason why Newfoundland's connections to the slave trade were not talked about more by more people. She also notes that universities and researchers actively choose to focus on different things. According to Norvey, "we can't have a complete history without every part being accounted for." Her memories still trigger the same feelings of love and respect for her mother, but now there is additional information— information enveloped by the uncomfortable realities of slavery.

Norvey adds molasses to her snickerdoodle recipe. Her fruitcakes, which she only started making since living in Newfoundland, also feature molasses. Knowing more about the history and varying stories behind her ingredients makes the baking process more meaningful and thought-provoking. She pays more respect to each ingredient and their journeys to get to us and into Newfoundland culture. She thinks of all the people who were hurt trying to get her a carton of molasses or a bag of cocoa. As we hold these ingredients and think about their potencies, we can have a much stronger connection to a product that once seemed so removed and far away from us. She asserts that these connections enrich everything.

When nine-year-old Norvey first stood by a Newfoundland beach, surrounded by swaths of family she had just met, she instantly felt at home. A feeling she had long yearned for in Michigan, but "there was no ocean." Norvey is hopeful that those who examine history will push more forgotten voices to the fore. These underrated and unspoken connections bind us all together with great flavour and a potent history.

Come From Away
XMC

I had dreamed about Newfoundland for longer than I have lived in the province. As a child, sitting in my Jamaican living room in the early 2000s, my family and I logged countless hours in front of the TV listening to Toni Marie Wiseman deliver segments on birthdays, anniversaries, and personal events like little Billy's first day of Grade 1 on the NTV Evening Newshour. My grandmother preferred to watch *The Young and the Restless* on NTV. When her soaps ended, NTV played until it was time for *Wheel of Fortune* and *Jeopardy*. As the years went on, my family developed a distant, mediated bond with Newfoundland.

    I needed to see and experience Newfoundland for myself. The day I was accepted into Memorial University, nothing could contain the jubilation emanating from my whole being. It was my time to see this disparate land wedged into my subconscious—so much so that I had hinged my hopes of the future on a tertiary education from Newfoundland. A place I had nothing in common with, or so I thought. I wanted to be in Newfoundland, to start a new life in this new place. The University's motto *Provehito in Altum* translates to "launch forth into the deep." That was exactly what I was doing. My yearning had come full circle. Like many who come to Newfoundland, I soon fell in love with everything about the island, the weather included.

    When it snowed in October, I freaked out. I assumed I had until winter before signs of snow. It was not rain, but still wet. Just how much snow was there going to be? Had I been too young to pay attention to the weather segments on NTV? Had I been forewarned? A frail hail rained on Jamaica once in my lifetime, my only prior winter precipitation experience.

I was less and less freaked out by seasonal changes once I had proper winter gear. I learned to enjoy snowshoeing, sliding on crazy carpets, ice skating, and cross-country skiing. My relationship with the land and the people on it strengthened. After less than a year, I could not picture myself anywhere else in the world.

I wanted to belong to Newfoundland.

No matter how many shots of Screech I chugged, or cods I kissed, I could not shake my foreign status in Newfoundland. I was an "other." I was not born in Newfoundland, which some say is the only way to be "of and from Newfoundland." However, it felt deeper than just where I was born. I realized, as my years in Newfoundland accumulated, that if you look a certain way, most people in the province believe you cannot be "of Newfoundland."

My dark skin seemed to mean that I did not belong here and never would. I experience this sense of othering each time someone assumes that today is my first day in the province. Newfoundlanders have created a phrase to ensure people feel like they do not belong, a phrase pierced by undiscussed xenophobia and Newfoundland nationalism. In Newfoundland and Labrador, xenophobic concerns are often dismissed as "ignorance" rather than outright racism. This means that the subject is rarely tackled head-on. The phrase has become world renowned: it is the title of the musical detailing the charitable actions of the townspeople of Gander, Newfoundland and Labrador, after dozens of planes were grounded there in the wake of 9/11.

The idea is that people who "come from away" cannot ever really belong emboldens the official, popular history of Newfoundland.

This history says that Newfoundland is an island in the middle of the North Atlantic Ocean, lined by untamed coastlines and surrounded by deep blue-black waters populated by the brave Irish, English, and French settlers who dared to live on the rock.

The phrase "come from away" erases the histories of the First Peoples of said rock and its mainland counterpart. It avoids the truth that the Scots, French, Irish, and English who colonized the province *came from away*. They took the land from the people who lived here for thousands of years before Europeans came upon the Newfoundland shorelines. The Beothuk, who no longer exist mainly because of genocide at the hand of the settlers of Newfoundland and from European diseases they had no immunity against, are not often considered when you think of Newfoundlanders. Anyone with melanin-rich skin is also omitted from the list, even if they were born in Newfoundland.

It pains my heart to learn there are only a few who get to belong. Those who look like the descendants of the Irish, English, and the French. Without question, they are "of Newfoundland." If you are black or brown, you will be marked as a "come from away."

There are a few nuances embedded in the term *come from away*. First is an innate and sometimes harmless curiosity. Newfoundlanders are perennially curious about where other people are from, whether a community on the island or outside the province. In Newfoundland, where you are from can have origins in how communities were settled and the isolated experiences spanning long periods. The white townie moving to the bay is considered from away, but still of Newfoundland. The white Torontonian, and those from other mainland locales who find themselves enraptured by the wiles of Newfoundland, are also, forever, from away. However, if they are in St. John's, outside of close-knit small outport communities, other Newfoundlanders may not automatically assume they do not belong. But one look at my Blackness often elicits the questions, "How long have you been here? Where are you from? Is this your first winter? You must come from away, a CFA?" Seemingly harmless curious questions take on a different, more ostracizing meaning in the context of race. An implicit othering takes place in this context.

Loving and living in a place that gives you a label that constantly reinforces the idea that you do not belong, and you never will, is excruciating. It is especially tough to feel good about calling that place home. A difficult balancing act must be struck, when ultimately all I want is to belong, to be one who can claim the distinction of being "of Newfoundland." I wished I had known of the xenophobic experiences I would endure in Newfoundland as I watched countless episodes of *Scenes of Newfoundland* as a child in Jamaica.

Learning that Black people were part of Newfoundland history, and of their erasure, complicates my feelings about being called a CFA. The shortened version stings no less. When I first heard the term, I considered it as charismatic as the other cheeky colloquial expressions used on the island. It seemed to me, back then, a subtle way to differentiate the visitor from the brave souls who dared call this place home. I have since discovered that *come from away* is a life sentence.

The realization that, even after a lifetime in Newfoundland, I might never be considered "of Newfoundland" because I did not have the look of the Irish, English, and French cuts deeply. My body shakes as I attempt to write about the unending xenophobia people who do not look like they are of English, Irish, and French descent face in the province. *Come from away* is the great forgetting in action: a powerful tool to cherry-pick and enforce the racist past on which this island and country were founded. Canada is still in an active state of colonization.

Canada and Newfoundland have erased their sordid pasts. History books, teachers, folklorists, journalists, literary writers, and historians—even the award-winning Newfoundland and Labrador tourism ad campaigns—have successfully crafted the exact image that they wanted the world to have of Canada and Newfoundland. They meticulously constructed their own histories, only telling the stories they deemed important.

Canada has polished a popular history that showcases the nation as a heroic actor at the end of slavery in North America by providing the underground railroad; Canada's most publicized ties to the transatlantic slave trade relate to setting slaves free, offering them land in Nova Scotia during the American Revolution. While this is a nice story, it is not the whole story. Slavery was legally practiced in British North America until 1834; enslaved Black people used the same underground railroad to go to the northern United States as they fled from their bondage in Canada. Canada does not publicize the racist historic immigration policies that denied entry to Black bodies. In the 1950s, Black Caribbean workers' entry to Canada was based on a candidate's exceptionalism and the country's need of cheap labour—never based on a desire to include Black bodies as permanent settlers. Black nurses had to have more exceptional qualifications than their white counterparts to be admitted entry to Canada. Non-white people needed to satisfy the Minister of Immigration that they were worthy immigrants. This same rigour was not applied to those entering Canada from countries whose population consisted of mostly white people. The absences and elisions of enforced inequalities in Canada's history render it a grand fabrication. The people who were scrubbed from 200 years of history before the creation of the underground railroad are the by-products of history's success.

I am saddened and honoured to learn that the place I call home, centuries ago other Black people did as well. That this information is being blatantly ignored is exasperating and offensive. These people had stories, families, love in Newfoundland. Knowing more about Newfoundland Black history makes my desire to belong, to be "of Newfoundland," even stronger. Attainable even.

I feel that I am "of Newfoundland" and, more importantly, that I can be "of Newfoundland," despite my Blackness. I want us to challenge history, turn the great forgetting on its head and stop the gatekeeping of the idea of *belonging*. Given the bloody colonial formation of this country and province, Black people, or anyone who wants to belong, should not have to make a case backed by history to belong.

If you live and die here, you get to say you are from here. This applies to the person, Black, Asian, or white, who just stepped onto the tarmac in St. John's, Gander, or Stephenville for the first time minutes or decades ago, who has decided to call this place home.

No one should be barred from belonging. It is wonderful to be "of Newfoundland." The ability to claim this rich history grounds an individual in this magical, incredible land.

New Frames for Newfoundland
XMC

Kassie Drodge of Paradise, Newfoundland and Labrador, is a Black Jamaican Newfoundlander who has lived in Newfoundland for most of her life. We talked about growing up Black in Newfoundland and what it is like to be Black in Newfoundland as an adult. Drodge is a master's student at the University of Ottawa. For her thesis, she explored the theoretical framework of ecowomanism in the Newfoundland fishery. Ecowomanism provided Drodge with a nuanced perspective of the fisheries, cod, and how women's bodies were treated under colonial systems. Newfoundland's historic and present-day connection to Black female bodies is of utmost importance to Drodge.

As more details about Newfoundland and Labrador Black history is revealed, Drodge believes, it will change what it means to be a Black Newfoundlander, whether that Black person was born here or not. As a Black Jamaican Newfoundlander, Drodge says it was always hard to introduce herself professionally as "from Newfoundland. I was taught the white colonial history that has been spread as fact." History that continues to erase people who look like her from the history books.

The information presented in the *Unearthed* documentary series, as well as public works by artists Bushra Junaid and Camille Turner, made Drodge aware of Newfoundland's involvement in the transatlantic slave trade. For Drodge, knowing about Newfoundland Black history creates more of a home for her in Newfoundland and a strengthened identity in the province. Like Black Nova Scotians who can trace their province's lineage of Blackness to early Black settlements such as Preston or Africville, Drodge too is now proud to introduce herself at academic conferences as a Black woman coming from a place with recognized and rich Black history. Drodge is grateful to have this new, more complete frame through which to analyze Newfoundland.

Drodge grew up with her white family. She comes from a long line of fishers. Her family did not have the wealth and social status of merchants on Water Street in St. John's, but they found some success after generations of struggle in the feudal Newfoundland fishery. "Everyone was a fisherman up until my Nan." Drodge is proud of her Newfoundland family. Her great-grandfather owned his fishing boat, which helped feed his family of eight children. "He would meet Portuguese fishermen. Trade fish for cigarettes. My great-aunt learned how to make Spanish rice from the Spanish. Now I study anthropology and I search through old documents and there's a note in the old family files, we had a little store, about sending the slave girl to the store to get something. And that's it, no one knows anything more." This makes me wonder how many other Newfoundland families have buried connections to the transatlantic slave trade?

Canada and Newfoundland are both complicit in this coverup. We use material things to highlight the parts of history that we wish to be reminded of: the underground railroad, countless fishing museums. History has been sanitized; the ingredient is dissociated from its roots. As one could say about the coconut in Newfoundland. The dried white fleshy parts of the coconut are the defining element of a snowball, a traditional Newfoundland confection that Drodge grew up with: "It's a family recipe, my grandmother makes it. She learned it from her grandmother. This cookie that is covered in dried coconut."

I imagine how the first coconut got to Newfoundland. A fruit that I have enjoyed in many ways both fresh and dried. Growing up in Jamaica, before packaged coconut powder became wildly available, we had a coconut tree in our yard. I remember watching my grandmother and then my mother grate the inside of the coconut into bowls after we drank the coconut water. They squeezed the milk out of the grated fruit to make rice and peas for Sunday dinner. The insides of another coconut cubed and toasted, were then covered in caramelized ginger and dropped onto a banana leaf to make my favourite traditional Jamaican confection, appropriately named drops.

In Newfoundland, the coconut in the traditional context has been whitewashed, partly because the history of how it became so prominent in the hearts and culture of Newfoundlanders has been forgotten. There is no connection to the distant countries where they grow and their histories. Though it is a cookie that looks like a ball of snow, calling it a *snowball* creates another disconnect from the coconut's roots. Drodge and I both hope that more conversations and learning will be done around less critically analyzed aspects of Newfoundland culture. As more information becomes available about Newfoundland's Black history, she says, it will strengthen Black Newfoundlanders' sense of belonging to the province.

Black people have always had the right to claim they belong to Newfoundland as much as white Newfoundlanders. Black people have always been here, they have helped shape the culture of this place, and they have ensured that generations of children were cared for in Newfoundland. It is now up to the world to accept and adjust their understanding of the Newfoundlander to encompass that.

Heather Reframes
HB

When Xaiver and I found out about W.H. and his remains unearthed from a cemetery in L'Anse au Loup, we wanted to find out more. What on earth was a Black man doing on a ship off the coast of Labrador in the early 1800s?

We have asked questions, and we have connected a few dots. Now we know that W.H. was one of many Black men working aboard ships off the coasts of Newfoundland and Labrador and docking in our ports. Newfoundland was *not* exempt from the terrible practice of slavery. Dinah, Cornelius, Rachel, Katherine, Sancho, Sarah, Jack, Nancy, and Stephen were enslaved Black people living and working as domestic servants in Newfoundland in the 1700s and 1800s. We know that there were likely many more Black people, enslaved and free, present in Newfoundland and Labrador over the centuries, but little documented evidence of them exists. That is because Black people, especially enslaved Black people, were not documented by Europeans as people. We know that slave ships, built to transport enslaved Black people from Africa to the New World, were built in Newfoundland. The *Sarah* was the best known of them.

Newfoundland's and the Caribbean's shared food traditions, such as salt cod, rum, and molasses, are products of the transatlantic slave trade. Salt cod from Newfoundland was a cheap protein that fuelled the work of enslaved Black people to make more rum and molasses. Salt cod, in fact, is a popular dish everywhere along the Atlantic triangle.

Because of the ubiquity of the transatlantic slave trade in colonialism, it would have been highly unusual for *no* Black people to be present in Newfoundland and Labrador. Poor fishers and their families in Newfoundland had difficult lives, but they were also part of a system that could not have functioned without the enslaved labour of Black people. That it is possible to be both exploited and an exploiter of others in a complex, worldwide system of trade is as true in 1700 as it is today.

I had simply assumed that none of my pale-skinned, blue-eyed Newfoundland ancestors would ever have encountered a Black person. But my British-Newfoundland ancestors would likely have crossed paths with Black people many times. They would have stood on the same busy wharves, as ships from all over the world docked in Newfoundland ports. Possibly, they worked on the same fishing, trading, or naval vessels. My relatives may have sold fish to merchants who held enslaved Black workers. Perhaps my ancestors buried Black people in their cemeteries.

Maybe my ancestors held enslaved Black people themselves.

History depends on who is telling the story. Afua Cooper puts it this way: "When a little voice comes in, and says, 'Well, how about this? The descendants of the people who were creating the narrative, their ancestors held slaves, held Africans in St. John's?' And those descendants, they aren't even a part of the story. So, could we just reframe the story or rewrite the story a little bit, even a little bit to include those voices?"

I am going to try to reframe our stories, by opening my eyes wider and casting my nets farther. Think about the food we eat, the items we consume every day. Where in the world did they come from? Whose hands might have made them? Are the people who make our everyday objects living lives of fairness and dignity today?

How do we see everyone around us in our everyday life, recognize their contributions, and help everyone to live a life of dignity on their own terms?

We met historians, archaeologists and other experts who are working tirelessly to bring to the surface parts of Newfoundland and Labrador's history that most of us have not thought much about. There is more exciting research to come, much of it from young and emerging Black historians and researchers.

We are going to continue asking questions and connecting more dots. We hope you do, too. Please use our book as a gateway to check out the amazing work done by those we talked to in our quest to learn more.

And then, when you need to drop anchor, all hands are welcome to come ashore in Black Harbour.

Xaiver Rethinks
XMC

As a Black Newfoundlander, I feel a sense of pride and a sense of worry. I am proud that people who look like me helped to shape this place. I have come to love Newfoundland so much more than I could have imagined as a child watching it on TV with my family thousands of miles away.

I now know that Black people were kept on this island against their will. Forced to do things that they did not want to do. But at the same time, they cared for generations of earlier settlers of the island of Newfoundland, and Newfoundlanders. Enslaved Black women held Newfoundland babies closely and soothed them when they were fussy. They cooked meals that strengthened whole families. Enslaved Black men worked on fish plantations; they fished cod.

While Black people have been excluded from the stories and the popular history, at one point they affected the culture of this island. Newfoundland was made into what it is today by many different people. They may not all look Irish, English, French, or Scottish and some of these people looked like me. I feel like less of an outsider when I walk along the rugged rocky coastline of the Avalon.

Although I am proud of the information compiled in this book from the work of those experts we have interviewed, I still worry that these histories will be forgotten. I believe in the power of forgetting. The purveyors of "History" have taught us what they deemed fit. So have the trusted local orators and the keepers of family secrets. They all erased the stories of the enslaved in Newfoundland at one point. Remembering and retelling these stories of the free and enslaved peoples in Newfoundland and Labrador is a powerful act of reconciliation with the erasure of their lives from known history.

Newfoundland is a part of Canada, a country with an ongoing history of an inability to make lasting and meaningful forms of reconciliation with the First Nations peoples and others who have been the focus of reconciliation efforts. I worry that this information will be disregarded and the lives of Sarah, Sancho, Rachel, Cornelius, Stephen, Nancy, Jack, Dinah, Katherine, W.H., and all those who remain unnamed will once again be forgotten. Without an emphasis on truthful and fervent questioning of Newfoundland culture and identity, past and present, I do worry that the past will repeat itself. At some point, these people will become lost once again. The history of the province will benefit by telling a more complete version of history.

I am not asking anyone to stop doing screech-ins. But I do want us to consider: why is it appropriate to baptize someone as a Newfoundlander with a by-product of slave labour?

Never stop making snowballs, but as you roll the ball into the shredded coconut, ask how this confection made its way into your family's culinary traditions.

Ships and shipyards put Newfoundland craftmanship on the map, but that expert craftsmanship was also harnessed to help facilitate the stealing and killing of millions of Africans. This employment of expert craftmanship was a community affair, a family affair.

Newfoundland was a British colony with lords and merchants; and the poor and oppressed struggled to survive. In Jamaica, over hundreds of years, the almighty Newfoundland cod ensured that the system of forced labour and exploitation of stolen enslaved Africans could continue in Jamaica. While the results of slave labour became staples in Newfoundland life, culture, society, and cuisine. A sense of

Newfoundland identity bloomed all the while slavery was practiced throughout Britain and its colonies. Remembering the role that Newfoundland and residents of Newfoundland played in the slave trade will not erase the known history. These are just some of the conversations we need to have.

Revisiting W.H.

Xaiver: We started our journey with W.H. We had a look at his pants and jacket. We were curious about how he got to the waters surrounding Labrador and in the community of L'Anse au Loup when there were no traces of other Black people in that area.

Heather: I was shocked to learn about W.H. I've lived here almost all my life and I'd never heard of him.

Xaiver: We wondered if he was alone, if he was the only Black person that had set foot on Newfoundland and Labrador soil during the early 1800s.

Heather: He wasn't alone, that's certain. Lots of Black people, we'll never know how many, moved in and out of Newfoundland and Labrador over the centuries.

Xaiver: We've written about some of them—Sarah, Sancho, Stephen, Nancy, Jack, Katherine, Dinah, Cornelius, and Rachel—and while we may never know their full stories and what brought them to Newfoundland and Labrador, we know that they were here from as early as the 1600s to John Ryan's will in the early 1800s.

Heather: And W.H.'s bones are stored in the basement of our provincial museum.

Xaiver: Maybe if kinship can be established, The Rooms might be able to turn over W.H.'s remains to someone who can properly bury him. Meanwhile, Memorial University is still researching W.H.'s clothing and belongings to see what more can be discovered.

Heather: It would be appropriate for him to find rest finally in death. What needs to be done to put W.H. to rest?

Xaiver: Right. It seems like W.H. is just another entry in The Rooms' catalogue. He's curated and stored like a piece of art. Except the artifacts related to his life aren't on permanent display; they too are hidden away. There's work being done to learn more about W.H.'s life, which is great. However, the tests that could be done, like DNA testing of W.H.'s teeth and bones, which would tell us conclusively where he was from, isn't being done. Why not? Does W.H. not deserve to find true rest? Neither of us would like W.H.'s story to end in the basement of a museum and never be talked about again.

While we wait to find out more about W.H., his discovery still has me wondering about how many more Black people passed through our province that weren't recorded or remembered. How many Black people contributed to making Newfoundland and Labrador?

Heather: We know of a few Black people buried in St. John's and possibly another man in Trinity.

Xaiver: How many more Black people are buried here, unmarked and unremembered? How much of Newfoundland culture to which Black people contributed has also been lost because of this Great Forgetting?

Heather: I'm thinking of Newfoundland and Labrador place names: Portugal Cove, Spanish Room, English Harbour ...

Xaiver: There's also a Kingston.

Heather: There's more to our story and more to our history than I'd been taught.

Xaiver: For me, it's been oddly comforting to know that this place that I do feel so akin to and drawn to wasn't just built by English, Irish, and French settlers. It makes me more at home in the province having access to all this new information and recognizing that Newfoundland did benefit from the labours of enslaved Black people and had a direct financial stake in the transatlantic slave trade, which affect the lives of millions of people to this day.

Heather: You know how in Newfoundland it seems like everyone seems to know each other, or knows someone who knows someone you know? Maybe our ancestors crossed paths—on a ship, on a wharf, in a back kitchen.

Xaiver: Back then, they probably wouldn't have had the chance to share a meal of salt cod and molasses buns. But we're here. We can share that meal for them now.

Dear W.H.
XMC

Dear W.H. I have known you now only a few years,
but in that time,
you have caused me and many people to think.
You have lived on the tip of my tongue.
I am honoured to help champion your legacy.

Dear W.H. I wonder
about your sons, daughters,
whether or not there were any.
Your mother, father, sister, brother
Your kin.
Of your lovers left behind.

Dear W.H. I yearn to learn
of your life before the seas.
What hobbies led you to become the immortalized sailor?
Or did you have no choice in your voyages
across the wide-open ocean,
in the trip that claimed your life?

Dear W.H. I long to know your stories.
I wish that textbooks were filled with your history,
of what led you to the coast of Labrador.
Tell me, W.H. what was it like as a Black sailor on board?
And from whence did you come?

Dear W.H. Your presence in Newfoundland and Labrador is profound.
Because of you, we have taken the time to know:
Sarah, Sancho, Nancy, Jack, Stephen, Katherine, Dinah, Rachel, Cornelius.
Thank you for being the catalyst.
Opening the door to discussions
of freedom and the enslavement of Black bodies
in Newfoundland and Labrador.
Thank you for living, and thank you for being here.

Dear W.H. I wish the world was eager
to lay you back to rest.
Your weary bones,
one day returned to your kin.
So, you may find peace.
These are my deepest desires for you, dear W.H.

Dear W.H. You are an inspiration.
Dear W.H. It is important that you know you do have a legacy.
One filled with discovery, action, curiosity, revolution and freedom.
You have helped stir the congealing remnants of Black history on this colonized land.
Thank you for all that you have done,
my dear W.H.

Black Harbour Timeline: Newfoundland and Labrador

1444: 235 Black Africans are sold to European owners in Lagos, Portugal. The Atlantic slave trade begins.

1490s: The Age of Discovery begins.

1497: John Cabot lands somewhere in Newfoundland, possibly Bonavista, and claims the New Found Lande for England.

1500-1530: Spanish and Portuguese ships and their crews begin fishing for cod in the North Atlantic Ocean waters around Newfoundland.

1500s: Basque, English, and French crews establish seasonal fishing stations on Newfoundland's coasts and on the south coast of Labrador.

1610: John Guy establishes the first year-round British colony in Newfoundland at Cupids.

1621: The Colony of Avalon in Ferryland, Newfoundland, is founded by Sir George Calvert.

1626: A port record in Southampton, England, indicates a ship stopped in Newfoundland and its captain purchases 80,000 fish and a slave.

1628: The first recorded sale of a Black African occurs in Canada. A nine-year-old boy from Madagascar is sold by British colonist David Kirke to a Quebec clerk.

1637: Sir David Kirke, known slave owner, has the rights of the Colony of Avalon in Newfoundland signed over to him.

1638: Kirke becomes governor of Newfoundland.

1662: The French set up a colony in Plaisance, now known as Placentia.

1677: A reference to a Black female slave in Placentia is found in a 1677 document.

1751: The first "slave ship" is built in Newfoundland.

1791: John Benger, prominent English settler in Ferryland, writes his last will and testament. In it, he declares that his family of enslaved Black people—Sarah and Sancho, and their children Jack, Nancy, and Stephen—are to be freed when he dies.

1763: The last battle of the Seven Years War between England and France cedes French colonies in North America, including Newfoundland, to England.

1788: The *Sarah*, a ship built to transport enslaved people and other cargo, is built somewhere in Newfoundland, and makes its maiden voyage from Newfoundland to Bristol, England.

1791: The *Sarah* delivers 190 enslaved Africans purchased in Bonny to Jamaica; 40 are lost during the voyage.

1792: The last of 19 ships built to transport enslaved people is built in Newfoundland.

1793: The *Calabar*, a ship built in Newfoundland to transport enslaved people loads 243 enslaved Africans bought in New Calabar; 208 survive the journey and are delivered to Montego Bay, Jamaica.

1793: The *Sarah* delivers 140 enslaved Africans purchased at Bonny to Kingston, Jamaica; 14 die during the voyage. The *Sarah* is shipwrecked after the enslaved Africans disembarked.

1799: The *Tonyn*, a ship built in Newfoundland to transport enslaved people, loads 326 enslaved Africans purchased near the Congo River; 299 survive and are delivered to Kingston, Jamaica.

Circa 1800: W.H. dies and is buried in L'Anse aux Loup, Labrador.

1804: A musician from Martinique, aboard a vessel commanded by a General Henesy or a General Henry, dies and is buried in Trinity, Newfoundland.

1808: On January 1, the Abolition Bill is passed by Britain. Trading in African slaves is declared to be "utterly abolished, prohibited and declared to be unlawful."

1814: John Ryan, a newspaper publisher living in St. John's, Newfoundland, writes his last will and testament. The will instructs that his slave, Dinah, be freed upon his death, but her children, Cornelius and Rachel, should continue to be enslaved by Ryan's family until they reach the age of 21.

1833: Slavery is abolished in the British empire.

1865: Slavery is abolished in the United States.

1940s and 1950s: American and Canadian Armed Forces create military bases in Newfoundland and Labrador, a strategic defence location in the North Atlantic. Black servicemen from those countries are posted there and socialize with local people.

1949: Newfoundland becomes the 10th Canadian province.

1987: W.H.'s remains are unearthed in L'Anse au Loup, Labrador.

1993: *The Black Atlantic*, a book and concept by Paul Gilroy, inspires researchers looking at the Black experience during the triangular trade and transatlantic slave trade.

2000s: More Black people, from Africa, the Caribbean, the United States, and elsewhere, immigrate to Newfoundland and Labrador for education and job opportunities and for humanitarian reasons. Several thousand Black Newfoundlanders and Labradorians are helping diversify the predominantly English-Irish population.

2020: W.H.'s uniform is displayed at The Rooms, as part of the exhibit "What Carries Us: Newfoundland and Labrador in the Black Atlantic," curated by Bushra Junaid.

Black Harbour Timeline: Jamaica

600-650: The Redware people arrive in Xaymaca.

800: The Arawakan-speaking people, the Tainos, arrive in Xaymaca.

1494: Christopher Columbus arrives in Xaymaca on his second voyage to the West Indies. Begins to colonize island for Spain.

1511: Peter Martyr d'Anghiera's *Decades* refers to Xaymaca as both "Jamaica" and "Jamica." The bastardization of the Indigenous name Jamaica is used to refer to the island.

1513: The Spanish bring the first Africans, taken from West Africa by the Spanish and the Portuguese, to Jamaica from the Iberian Peninsula.

1655: The British invade Jamaica and begin to battle with Spain for control of the island. The Spanish free the island's enslaved Africans.

1655-1670: Hundreds of enslaved Africans revolt in Jamaica. They mount a resistance by "Spanish negroe" Lubolode Serras and others.

1663: The first General Elections are held in Jamaica in December. First in the New World, they are neither representative or democratic.

1670s-1680s: The enslaved population grows to around 10,000, with 57 sugar plantations counted in Jamaica by 1673.

1673: Hundreds of enslaved Africans from Coromantee revolt. Lobby's estate, St. Ann's parish, Jamaica.

1685: Hundreds of enslaved Africans revolt in July. Grey's estate, Guanaboa Vale, Jamaica.

1690: Hundreds of enslaved Africans revolt in July led by Cudjoe the elder. Sutton's estate, Clarendon parish, Jamaica.

1692: Earthquake devastates city of Port Royal.

1730-1740: Thousands of enslaved Africans fight in the First Maroon War against the British.

1739: Four hundred and thirty sugar plantations in Jamaica.

1739/1740: The Maroons' guerrilla warfare leads them to victory in the First Maroon War. They gain their political autonomy from Britain to create a nation within Jamaica.

1760: Hundreds of thousands of enslaved Africans, dominated by Coromantee people, fight in Tacky's revolt, originating in St. Mary's parish, Jamaica, on Easter Monday. Revolt spread widely through island.

1766: A ship built in Newfoundland to transport enslaved people, the *Antelope*, loads 396 enslaved Africans bought from Bight of Biafra and Gulf of Guinea Islands, port unspecified. Seven die during the voyage. The remaining 289 are delivered to Jamaica.

1766: Thousands of enslaved Coromantee people revolt in Westmoreland parish, Jamaica.

1766: The *Roebuck*, built in Newfoundland to transport enslaved people, delivers 310 stolen Africans purchased from the Gold Coast to Jamaica. Twenty die during the voyage.

1776: Thousands of enslaved Africans revolt in July. Led by Sam, Charles, Caesar, and others in Hanover parish, Jamaica.

1788: The *Sarah*, a ship built to transport enslaved people and other cargo, is built somewhere in Newfoundland, and makes its maiden voyage from Newfoundland to Bristol, England.

1790: The *Sarah* purchases enslaved Africans at Cameroon's River, Bimbia, and Calabar. Of the 257 enslaved Africans that boarded the *Sarah*, 80 die during the voyage and those who survived were delivered to Jamaica.

1791: The *Sarah* delivers 190 enslaved Africans purchased in Bonny to Jamaica. Forty are lost during the voyage.

1791/1792: Hundreds of enslaved Africans participate in island-wide unrest after news of the Haitian Revolution spreads across Jamaica.

1793: The *Calabar*, a ship built in Newfoundland to transport enslaved people, loads 243 enslaved Africans bought in New Calabar; 208 survive the journey. They are delivered to Montego Bay, Jamaica.

1793: The *Sarah* delivers 140 enslaved Africans purchased at Bonny to Kingston, Jamaica; 14 die during the voyage. The *Sarah* is shipwrecked after the enslaved Africans disembark.

1795/1796: From July to March, hundreds of enslaved Africans participate in the Second Maroon War in Trelawny and St. James's parish, Jamaica.

1799: The *Tonyn*, a ship built in Newfoundland to transport enslaved people, loads 326 enslaved Africans purchased near the Congo River; 299 survive and are delivered to Kingston, Jamaica.

1806: Dozens of enslaved Africans revolt. Plot in St. George's parish, Jamaica.

1808: On January 1, the Abolition Bill is passed by Britain. Trading in African slaves is declared to be "utterly abolished, prohibited and declared to be unlawful."

1808: Hundreds of enslaved Africans participate in the mutiny of the Second West India Regiment and plot in Kingston, Jamaica.

1815: On Christmas Day, hundreds of enslaved Africans revolt, an Ibo-led plot, in St. Elizabeth's parish, Jamaica.

1823/1824: Thousands of enslaved Africans revolt. Widespread plots and unrest, especially in Hanover parish, Jamaica, where it is properly called the Argyle War.

1831/1832: Christmas. Hundreds of thousands fight in the Baptist War in western Jamaica, led by Samuel Sharpe and others.

1833: Slavery is abolished in the British empire.

1834: Enslaved Africans in Jamaica are "emancipated," but enter exploitative apprenticeships under their former owners.

1838: August 1. Jubilation breaks out as approximately 311,000 previously enslaved Africans celebrate the Emancipation Declaration in Jamaica, declaring their full freedom from slavery.

1845: The first Indian people arrive in Jamaica as indentured servants.

1854: The first Chinese people arrive in Jamaica as indentured servants

1865: Civil unrest culminates in the Morant Bay Rebellion led by Paul Bogle and others. Britain suspends the Jamaican Assembly.

1914: Marcus Garvey establishes the United Negro Improvement Association (UNIA).

1944: The first general elections under universal adult suffrage.

1962: August 6. Jamaica becomes an independent nation.

References and Further Reading

WORKS CITED

Bannister, Jerry. *The Rule of the Admirals: Law, Custom, and Naval Government in Newfoundland, 1699-1832*. University of Toronto Press, 2003.

Bolster, W. Jeffrey. *Black Jacks: African American Seamen in the Age of Sail*. Harvard University Press, 1997.

Cooper, Afua. *The Hanging of Angelique: The Untold Story of Canadian Slavery and the Burning of Old Montreal*. HarperCollins, 2006.

Fortin, Jeffrey A. "'Blackened beyond Our Native Hue': Removal, Identity and the Trelawney Maroons on the Margins of the Atlantic World, 1796-1800." *Citizenship Studies* 10, no. 1(2006): 5-34.

Fuller, Harcourt and Jada Ben Torres. "Investigating the 'Taíno' Ancestry of the Jamaican Maroons: A New Genetic (DNA), Historical, and Multidisciplinary Analysis and Case Study of the Accompong Town Maroons." *Canadian Journal of Latin American and Caribbean Studies* 43 (2018): 47-78.

Gaulton, Barry C. and Catherine Hawkins. "Interim Report: Ferryland (CgAf-2). Permit # 15.20." 2015.

Gaulton, Rick. "Early Historic Beothuk Indian Evidence from Ferryland, Newfoundland (CgAf-2)." BA Honour's essay, Memorial University of Newfoundland, 2001.

Lalah, Robert. "Codfish Fears Conquered." *The Jamaica Gleaner*, May 19, 2009. http://old.jamaica-gleaner.com/gleaner/20090519/life/life1.html.

Mathias, Cathy and Sonja M. Jerkic. "Investigating W.H.: A Nineteenth Century Burial from L'Anse au Loup, Labrador." *Canadian Journal of Archaeology* 19 (1995): 101-16.

Miller, Aaron F. "Avalon and Maryland: A Comparative Historical Archaeology of the Seventeenth Century New World Provinces of the Lords Baltimore (1621-1644)." PhD diss., Memorial University of Newfoundland, 2013.

Prowse, D.W. *A History of Newfoundland*. Boulder, 2002. First published by MacMillan and Co., London, 1895.

Richardson, David, ed. *Bristol, Africa, and the Eighteenth-Century Slave Trade to America*. Vol. 4: The Final Years, 1770-1807. Bristol Record Society Publications, Vol. 47, 1996.

Rose, George A. *Cod: The Ecological History of the North Atlantic Fisheries*. Breakwater Books, Ltd., 2007.

Ryan, John. "CAUTION." *Royal Gazette* (Saint John, NB), December 24, 1806. In *Black Slavery in the Maritimes: A History in Documents*, by Harvey Amani Whitfield. Broadview Press, 2018.

Snooks, Gina and Sonja Boon. "Salt Fish and Molasses: Unsettling the Palate in the Spaces between Two Continents." *The European Journal of Life Writing* 6 (2017): 218-41. https://ejlw.eu/article/view/31492/28851.

Tye, Diane. "A Poor Man's Meal: Molasses in Atlantic Canada." *Food, Culture and Society* 11, no. 3 (2015): 335-53.

Williams, Heather Andrea. "How Slavery Affected African American Families." Freedom's Story, TeacherServe©. National Humanities Center. June 1, 2002. https://nationalhumanitiescenter.org/tserve/freedom/1609-1865/essays/aafamilies.htm.

Will of John Benger of Ferryland, Newfoundland, North America. Records of the Prerogative Court of Canterbury, PROB 11/1227/235, The National Archives (UK).

JAMAICAN HISTORY REFERENCES

Bilby, Kenneth M. "Maroon Autonomy in Jamaica." *Cultural Survival*, April 15, 2010. https://www.culturalsurvival.org/publications/cultural-survival-quarterly/maroon-autonomy-jamaica.

Black, Clinton V. *History of Jamaica*. Longman, 1988.

Brown, Lynn. M. "The Obscured History of Jamaica's Maroon Societies." *JSTOR Daily* 2016. https://daily.jstor.org/maroon-societies-in-jamaica/.

Carlyle, Thomas. *Oliver Cromwell's Letters and Speeches: With Elucidations*. Wiley and Putnam, 1845.

Chopra, Ruma. "Maroons and Mi'kmaq in Nova Scotia, 1796-1800." *Acadiensis: Journal of the History of the Atlantic Region* 46, no. 1 (2017): 5-23.

Craton, Michael. *Testing the Chains: Resistance to Slavery in the British West Indies*. Cornell University Press, 1982.

Cundall, Frank. *Historic Jamaica*. Ballantyne, Hanson and Co. London, 1915.

Day, Chris. "The Morant Bay Rebellion, 1865." *The National Archives*, 2022. https://blog.nationalarchives.gov.uk/the-morant-bay-rebellion-october-1865/.

Ehrengardt, Thibault. *The History of Jamaica from 1494 to 1836*. Dread Editions, 2015.

Haile, Shenhat. Investigating Discourses of Indigeneity and Taino Survival in Jamaica. *Caribbean Quilt* 6, no. 1 (2021): 26-35.

Hutton, Clinton. Review of *The Killing Time: The Morant Bay Rebellion in Jamaica*, by Gad Heuman. *Social and Economic Studies* 44, no. 1 (1995): 191-205.

Klein, Herbert S. "The English Slave Trade to Jamaica, 1782-1808." *The Economic History Review* 31, no. 1 (1978): 25-45.

Kopytoff, Barbara Klamon. "The Early Political Development of Jamaican Maroon Societies." *The William and Mary Quarterly* 35, no. 2 (1978): 287-307.

Lockett, James D. "The Deportation of the Maroons of Trelawny Town to Nova Scotia, then Back to Africa." *Journal of Black Studies* 30, no. 1 (1999): 5-14.

Rampersad, Sabrina R. "Targeting the Jamaican Ostionoid: The Blue Marlin Archaeological Project." *Caribbean Quarterly* 55, no. 2 (2009): 23-42.

Robinson, Kavion. *Out of Many, One People: The Story of Jamaica*. Self-published, 2019.

Sivapragasam, Michael. "After the Treaties: A Social, Economic and Demographic History of Maroon Society in Jamaica, 1739-1842." PhD diss., University of Southampton, 2018.

Tortello, Rebecca. "Pieces of the Past: The Arrival of the Africans." *The Jamaica Gleaner*, 2004. https://old.jamaica-gleaner.com/pages/history/story0059.htm.

Wright, M.L. "The Accompong Town Maroons: Past and Present." *Creativity and Resistance*. Smithsonian Institution Traveling Exhibition Service (SITES) and Center for Folklore and Cultural Heritage, 1999. https://folklife.si.edu/resources/maroon/educational_guide/63.htm.

FURTHER READING

Aronson, Marc and Marina Budhos. *Sugar Changed the World: A Story of Magic, Spice, Slavery, Freedom and Science*. Houghton Mifflin Harcourt Publishing Company, 2017.

Cole, Desmond. *The Skin We're In: A Year of Black Resistance and Power*. Anchor Canada, 2022.

English, Christopher. "Newfoundland's Early Laws and Legal Institutions: From Fishing Admirals to the Supreme Court of Judicature in 1791-92." *Manitoba Law Journal* 23 (1996): 57-78. https://canlii.ca/t/sgcs.

"The Fishery and Fish Trade, 1500-1800." Memorial University, Grenfell Campus. Last updated January 10, 2021. https://www2.grenfell.mun.ca/nfld_history/nfld_history_fishery.htm.

Gilroy, Paul. *The Black Atlantic: Modernity and Double Consciousness*. Verso, 1993.

Gutman, Herbert G. *The Black Family in Slavery and Freedom, 1750-1925*. Vintage Books, 1976.

Harris, Melanie L. *Ecowomanism: African American Women and Earth Honoring Faiths*. Orbis Books, 2017.

Kurlansky, Mark. *Cod: A Biography of the Fish That Changed the World*. Walker Publishing Company, 1997.

Major, Kevin. *As Near to Heaven by Sea: A History of Newfoundland and Labrador*. Penguin Books Canada Ltd., 2001.

Pope, Peter E. *Fish into Wine: The Newfoundland Plantation in the Seventeenth Century*. Omohundro Institute and University of North Carolina Press, 2004.

Tuck, James A. "Archaeology at Ferryland, Newfoundland." *Newfoundland Studies* 9, no. 2 (1993): 294-310.

WEBSITES

The Slave Voyages Database: slavevoyages.org

Heritage Newfoundland & Labrador: heritage.nf.ca

Jamaica Information Service: jis.gov.jm

Black Maple Magazine: blackmaplemagazine.com

Newfoundland Shipbuilding: newfoundlandshipbuilding.com

The British Empire: britishempire.co.uk

Caribbean Compass: caribbeancompass.com

Appendix 1:
NEWFOUNDLAND-BUILT SHIPS IN THE TRANSATLANTIC SLAVE TRADE

Year ship arrived with enslaved people in New World	Date ship constructed	Name of ship	Location where enslaved people were purchased	Principal place ship landed	Enslaved Africans boarding	Enslaved Africans arrival at 1st port
1758	1751	Betsey	Bance/Bunce Island	Charleston	269	230
1759	1751	Betsey	Sierra Leone estuary	Charleston	257	220
1760	1751	Betsey	Africa, port unspecified	St. Kitts	230	197
1773	1768	Wasp	Calabar	St. Kitts	78	69
1776		Antelope	Bight of Biafra and Gulf of Guinea Islands	Jamaica	403	396
1776	1752	Roebuck	Gold Coast	Jamaica	330	310
1776	1774	Swallow	Saint-Louis	Mississippi	119	93
1779	1763	Friends	Cape Coast Castle	Trinidad and Tobago	25	23
1787	1779	Maria	Anomabu	Havana	240	230
1787	1786	Chance				
1790	1788	Sarah	Cameroon's River	Jamaica	256	176
1791	1785	Maria	Bassa	Grenada	80	79
1791	1788	Sarah	Bonny	Jamaica	231	190
1972	1787	Betsey	Bonny	Grenada	248	226
1792	1778	Morning Star	Sierra Leone estuary		56	

HEATHER BARRETT was born and raised in St. John's, Newfoundland and Labrador, where she still lives with her family. She holds a Bachelor of Music from Memorial University of Newfoundland and a Master of Arts in Journalism from Western University in London, Ontario.

Heather is a journalist and storyteller, and an international award-winning radio documentary producer. She is also a long-time producer and host with the Canadian Broadcasting Corporation, based in St. John's. When she is not telling stories, Heather is an avid knitter and an avid runner, but not at the same time. This is Heather's first book.

About the Authors

XAIVER MICHAEL CAMPBELL is a Jamaican-born writer who has been living in Newfoundland and Labrador for over a decade. These islands are quite different, but Xaiver feels that living in Jamaica prepared him for life on the Rock. Minus the snow, sleet, and lack of sun—the people are equally warm and friendly. Xaiver loves the outdoors and when not writing, doing childcare, baking, playing, or watching basketball, he can be found swimming in the ponds all across the Newfoundland, and camping on and hiking the East Coast Trail.

His fiction has been published in *The Malahat Review, Riddle Fence,* and several anthologies. His second play, *One Name* was workshopped by Halifax Theatre for Young People. Xaiver's non-fiction work concerns the lives of enslaved and freed Black people in early Newfoundland settlements.

CBC, the Canadian Broadcasting Corporation, for permitting us to use some of the material gathered for the CBC project in this book.

Our early readers—Amanda Bittner, Amelia Harris, Ann Martin, Paul Shea, Jack Harris, Lisa Moore, Natalie Spracklin, Doug Letto, and Colin Moore—for their invaluable counsel.

The crew at Boulder Books for asking us to write this book and for their excellent guidance and support, and especially our amazing editor, Stephanie Porter, who, with additional editing from Iona Bulgin, pulled this book together.

Heather would like to thank her family—Chris, Joe, Ella, and Judy—for their love and support.

Xaiver would like to thank the Creator, Mummy, Grandma, Daniel, Natalie, and Sarah for their love and support.

Xaiver would also like to offer his co-author, Heather, an eternal amount of thank yous for her giving spirit and steadfast dedication to the telling of these stories of Black Harbour and about Newfoundland. Thank you, thank you, thank you!

Acknowledgements

We are grateful for the work and for the generous time given to us by the people that we interviewed for this book. Please check out their work online, on bookshelves, in galleries, and in their communities. They are: Afua Cooper, Emily Davidson, Kassie Drodge, Barry Gaulton, Dale Jarvis, Neil Kennedy, Charmaine Nelson, Donna Norvey, Kevin Toope, and Camille Turner.

We also thank:

The staff at the Colony of Avalon in Ferryland, Newfoundland and Labrador.

The staff at The Rooms, Newfoundland and Labrador's provincial museum, art gallery, and archives, in St. John's.

The staff at the Mercado de Escravos in Lagos, Portugal.

Dr. Sonja Boon at Memorial University and Bushra Junaid, artist, writer, and curator.

CBC Newfoundland and Labrador. This book grew out of a CBC project called *Unearthed: Slavery in Newfoundland and Labrador*. *Black Harbour* would not exist without it.

Enslaved African deaths onboard	Ship captain	Ship owners	Voyage outcome
0	James Morris	Christopher Kelley, Pierce O'Donnell	enslaved delivered for original owners, subsequent fate unknown
8	Richard Bennett	Neale Napleton	enslaved delivered for original owners, subsequent fate unknown
1	Thomas Keen	Thomas Keen	enslaved delivered for original owners, subsequent fate unknown
1	Thomas Keen	Thomas Keen	enslaved delivered for original owners, subsequent fate unknown
10			

Data gathered from the Slave Voyages Database.

Appendix 2:
NEWFOUNDLAND-BUILT SHIPS IN THE INTRA-AMERICAN SLAVE TRADE

Year ship arrived with enslaved people in New World	Date ship constructed	Name of ship	Where enslaved people were purchased	Principal place ship landed	Enslaved Africans boarding	Enslaved Africans at 1st port
1764	1756	Mary	Barbados	Essequibo	6	6
1764	1761	Greyhound	Barbados	Jamaica	174	166
1765	1750	General Wolfe	Dominica	Grenada	13	12
1765	1750	General Wolfe	St. Kitts	Grenada	13	12
Total Enslaved Africans Delivered and Deaths					**206**	**196**

Enslaved African deaths onboard	Ship captain	Ship owners	Voyage outcome
	William Ramsay	William Ramsay	human agency thwarted transport; cut off by Africans from shore
9	Gerard Preston, John Foulkes	James Penny, Moses Benson, Peter Rigby, John Backhouse, William Rutson, Thomas Dixon	enslaved delivered for original owners, subsequent fate unknown
31	John Foulkes	James Penny, Moses Benson, Peter Rigby, John Backhouse, William Rutson, Thomas Dixon	captured by French, enslaved disembarked in Americas
35	John Simpson, William Hutcheson	James Rogers, Patrick Fitzhenry	enslaved delivered for original owners, subsequent fate unknown
14	James Crean Hunt, William Blake	James Rogers, James Laroche, John Goodrich, Richard Fydell, Richard Blake, John Purnell	shipwrecked after disembarkation
26	John Spencer	Henry Keowen Hunter, Robert Hunter	captured by French, enslaved disembarked in Americas
31	Timothy Boardman	Thomas Earle, Francis Holland, Joseph Caton, William Earle, John Smale, Ralph Fisher, William Molyneux, Edmond Molyneux, Thomas Jolly	enslaved delivered for original owners, subsequent fate unknown
	R. Andrews	John Dawson	captured by French, enslaved disembarked in Americas
31	Timothy Boardman	Robert Bent	captured by French, enslaved disembarked in Americas
7	Richard Andow		enslaved delivered for original owners, subsequent fate unknown
29	Thomas Conning Smith	Patrick Fairweather, James Seddon, John Gibbons, John Platt, John Rackham, John Vose, William Sherwood	enslaved delivered for original owners, subsequent fate unknown
	Richard Martin	William Harper, Daniel Backhouse, John Tarleton	ship condemned before enslaved people embarked, 341 intended captives
4			enslaved delivered for original owners, subsequent fate unknown
27	James Towers	Thomas Bailey, Michael Taylor, Ralph Cantrell, Roger Grimshaw	shipwrecked or destroyed after enslaved disembarked
569			

Data gathered from the Slave Voyages Database.

Appendix 1 cont'd
NEWFOUNDLAND-BUILT SHIPS IN THE TRANSATLANTIC SLAVE TRADE

Year ship arrived with enslaved people in New World	Date ship constructed	Name of ship	Location where enslaved people were purchased	Principal place ship landed	Enslaved Africans boarding	Enslaved Africans arrival at 1st port
1792	1781	Fly	Badagry/Apa		113	
1792	1783	Torbay	Ambriz	Grenada	245	236
1792	1783	Torbay	Africa, port unspecified	Martinique	359	328
1793	1785	Friendship	New Calabar	Jamaica, Montego Bay	243	208
1793	1788	Sarah	Bonny	Jamaica, Kingston	154	140
1793	1787	Betsey	Africa, port unspecified	Jacmel	309	283
1794	1787	Ocean	Bight of Biafra and Gulf of Guinea Islands, Cameroon, Gabon	Barbados	359	328
1794	1792	Good Hope				
1795	1787	Ocean	West Central Africa and St. Helena	Basse-Terre	359	328
1797	1788	Swallow	Cape Coast Castle	St. Croix	105	98
1797	1779	Tonyn	Calabar	St. Croix	343	314
1799	1787	Ocean				
1799	1788	Swallow	Cape Coast Castle	Zion Hill, Tobago	61	57
1799	1779	Tonyn	Congo River	Jamaica, Kingston	326	299
Total Enslaved Africans Delivered and Deaths					**5,798**	**5,058**

Enslaved African deaths onboard	Ship captain	Ship owners	Voyage outcome
39	Wm. Cogill	Richard Oswald, Alexander Grant, John Sargent, Augustus Boyd	enslaved delivered for original owners, subsequent fate unknown
37	Robert Deas	Robert Oswald, Grant Nayr, John Sergent, Augustus Boyd	enslaved delivered for original owners, subsequent fate unknown; ship returned direct to Africa after bringing enslaved to the Americas
33	Robert Deas	Robert Oswald, Grant Nayr, John Sergent, Augustus Boyd	enslaved delivered for original owners, subsequent fate unknown
9	James McCreight	Alex Nottingham, William James, Gill Slater, Edward Grayson, Thos Spencer Dunn	enslaved delivered for original owners, subsequent fate unknown
7	Mungo Wright	David Hamilton	enslaved delivered for original owners, subsequent fate unknown
20	Thomas Gullan	D. Hamilton, Coghlan	enslaved delivered for original owners, subsequent fate unknown
26	H. Beard, Henry Mosset Mallard	Js. Mather	enslaved delivered for original owners, subsequent fate unknown
	J.R. Wood, Richard Wood	P. Joliffe (Jr.)	shipwrecked, enslaved people perished with ship
10	Dennison	John Tunno	enslaved delivered for original owners, subsequent fate unknown
	James Millbanke	John Hodgson, Thomas Hodgson (Jr.)	ship condemned before enslaved people boarded, 60 intended captives
80	John Goodrich	James Rogers, James Laroche, John Goodrich, Richard Fydell, Richard Blake, John Powell (Jr.)	enslaved delivered for original owners, subsequent fate unknown
1	Charles Sloper	Jonathon Nash, William Jenkins, Charles Sloper	enslaved delivered for original owners, subsequent fate unknown
41	John Goodrich	James Rogers, James Laroche, John Goodrich, Richard Fydell, Richard Blake, John Purnell, Samuel Fydell	enslaved delivered for original owners, subsequent fate unknown
22	John Spencer	Henry K. Hunter, Robert Hunter	enslaved delivered for original owners, subsequent fate unknown
	William Stewart, William Fitzsimons	James Rogers, William Stewart, Thomas Walker	human agency stopped transport, enslaved people returned to Old World